T0157867

Power To Transform The NATURAL By The SUPERNATURAL

Dr. Raha Mugisho

Order this book online at www.trafford.com
or email orders@trafford.com

Most Trafford titles are also available at major online book retailers.

© Copyright 2012 Dr. Raha Mugisho.
All rights reserved. No part of this publication may be reproduced, stored in a retrieval
system, or transmitted, in any form or by any means, electronic, mechanical, photocopying,
recording, or otherwise, without the written prior permission of the author.

Printed in the United States of America.

ISBN: 978-1-4669-3735-2 (sc)
ISBN: 978-1-4669-3734-5 (e)

Trafford rev. 05/10/2012

 www.trafford.com

North America & international
toll-free: 1 888 232 4444 (USA & Canada)
phone: 250 383 6864 ◆ fax: 812 355 4082

Do not ask my race, my education, my title, my origin; just believe and you shall see the glory of God. God is not a man that He would lie or a son of man that He could repent; He shall do whatever He said. He is faithful and honest, just believe and you will see the glory of God.

This is a best gift you may offer to yourself and to those that you really love; read this book lesson by lesson, meditate upon the Word and you will get the revelation which will cause you to understand and to stand in the supernatural.

I believe with all my heart that as long you are reading this book with a thirsty heart, I am sure God shall perform your expected miracle. The picture you have in your mind, God will make it to come true.

The patriarch of FAITH
Dr. RAHA MUGISHO
THE KING DAVID

CONTENTS

2011/02/12 09:14

DEDICATION

I dedicate this book to ABIGAIL and to my friends, DALLAS K, BODO PAMBU, RUNIGA LUGERERO. You joined together with me praying for my victory and my stability. From the bottom of my heart I am very grateful for your goodness and for all support you brought to me. Receive your blessings from the King David in Jesus' Name.

ACKNOWLEDGEMENTS

By this action I want to acknowledge my spiritual sons and daughters, MESCHACK AND AMANI CIBAMBO, TETE BANGAMWABO, MWEZE KASONGO, PEDRO AND MAPENDO ZINGIRE NTAMBUKA, THEODORE BIDUDU, TETE TANDO, BACHILEMBA DANIEL, BUHENWA PRINCESSE, MARY NYAMWIZA, MAPENDO AND AMANI BASHIGE, my partners, DALLAS K, NEEMA SIKETENDA, RUSS MOYER, STEVE FORTOSIS, JACQUES KILUWE, TANDO GODEFROID, LEON SANGARA, and JOHN KIDIGI.

The burden you support in this work of God is not in vain; God will repay all the sacrifices you made to bring me to another dimension.

Because of your support I was able to go ahead till I got seven elevations from God. May you find in my words the manifestation of my gratitude.

My success was your joy and my pains were nothing compared to the support you offered to me.

Be blessed

INTRODUCTION

THE SUPERNATURAL IS FOR
THOSE WHO UNDERSTAND AND STAND

MARK 11: NEW INTERNATIONAL VERSION

> [22]"Have faith in God," Jesus answered. [23]"Truly[f] I tell you, if anyone says to this mountain, 'Go, throw yourself into the sea,' and does not doubt in their heart but believes that what they say will happen, it will be done for them. [24]Therefore I tell you, whatever you ask for in prayer, believe that you have received it, and it will be yours. [25]And when you stand praying, if you hold anything against anyone, forgive them, so that your Father in heaven may forgive you your sins."

Faith is the key word in the supernatural reality; here the dream becomes reality and the idea finds its realization. Have faith in God and then claim your rights to the throne of God. The supernatural is for the children of God. Being in the supernatural, I am in the good place to recover all that the devil steals. In the supernatural we walk by faith, destroying all the strongholds of the devils in Jesus' name.

DO NOT FEAR; DO NOT DOUBT

RESIST THE DEVIL

ATTACK THE DEVIL AND DESTROY HIS STRONGHOLDS

DO NOT GIVE UP

CONFESS THE WORD OF FAITH

PROCLAIM YOUR VICTORY

TAKE YOUR PROPERTY IN THE SUPERNATURAL

THANK GOD BECAUSE HE WON THE BATTLE FOR YOU

We know that all words spoken from the mouth of our LORD JESUS are true and are the basic elements through which we build this living tabernacle—this temple of the Holy Spirit. Jesus is God, so put away all vain discussion concerning His identity. His spoken word is God's spoken word. If you refuse the divinity of Jesus, there is no way you will succeed in the supernatural reality with God.

> 1 John 5; 20 [20]And we know that the Son of God is come, and hath given us an understanding, that we may know him that is true, and we are in him that is true, even in his Son, Jesus Christ. This is the true God, and eternal life.
>
> John 1; 1-4, [1]In the beginning was the Word, and the Word was with God, and the Word was God.
>
> [2]The same was in the beginning with God.
>
> [3]All things were made by him; and without him was not anything made that was made.

[4]In him was life; and the life was the light of men.

Hebrews 1. [8]But unto the Son he saith, 'Thy throne, O God, is forever and ever: a sceptre of righteousness is the sceptre of thy kingdom.'

Colossians 1: [13]Who hath delivered us from the power of darkness, and hath translated us into the kingdom of his dear Son:

[14]In whom we have redemption through his blood, even the forgiveness of sins:

[15]Who is the image of the invisible God, the firstborn of every creature:

[16]For by him were all things created, that are in heaven, and that are in earth, visible and invisible, whether they be thrones, or dominions, or principalities, or powers: all things were created by him and for him:

[17]And he is before all things, and by him all things consist.

[18]And he is the head of the body, the church: who is the beginning, the firstborn from the dead; that in all things he might have the preeminence.

[19]For it pleased the Father that in him should all fulness dwell

1

SUPERNATURAL REALITIES WITH GOD

If you do not understand you cannot stand. You may think that you grasp the truth but in the sight of God's system you are caught up in a distraction. The supernatural is diametrically different from the natural. It means that there is a change; you who are natural become supernatural. The law of attraction is accomplished by a movement from the higher to the lower; when it moves from the bottom upward, it becomes supernatural. It does not seem normal to the human understanding. Elijah was caught up in the sight of Elisha; Jesus was caught up in the sight of his disciples. These movements were done by the power of God; and, by the Word of God, we know that the church will be caught up. It was the opposite movement, down to up like a plane that moves from the runway upward by human technology.

Which element can release someone to enter into the supernatural? This is not another thing than the blood of Christ. The blood is needed, and without the blood nothing can bring the migration from the natural to the supernatural. God, to make a powerful man, offered his own blood. Satan, to destroy the power of this human, polluted this blood, training the man to sin because the wages of sin is death. When anybody sins, they destroy themselves by partaking of death. Why are pagan people not able to stand it when any relative dies? It is because the blood has not been applied, so if we do not understand the impact of the blood and how it works in our favor, our victory can be temporary and not permanent. The devil also requires blood for promotion, and he asks it from his agents, not once but in all great events, and above all these, his agents have to give themselves over to evil to be appointed. But in the sight of God we know that the wages of sin is death. Because of the history of human transgression God required the system of bloodshed till the advent of our Lord Jesus, who gave himself once for all and, for whoever believes these receive the power of adoption.

John 1.12 Once was given to God the powerful blood of his begotten Son, Jesus; in him we have victory and adoption as sons and daughter of God. Every time we drink by faith the blood of Jesus and we eat his body we dwell in the supernatural area; no force of the devil can harm us and we have the right to confess and to declare all that God said in our favor. God is using life to secure his people but the devil is using death. God is using love but the devil is using hatred. And to gain access to drink the blood of Jesus and his body we must be holy, walking by faith and love. Therefore by this blood we pass from flesh to the spirit, from natural to supernatural (Romans 5).

Israel could not have the deliverance without passing through the process of the Passover blood, so when they finished this process, they saw how they received divine protection, the provision of God, the sign of wonder day and night. They passed from weakness to power and no enemy could stand before them as long they were walking according to the will of God. The use of the blood for sacrifice continued to purify them for alliances and for sacrifices till the advent of the Lord Jesus, the Lamb of God offered once for all as the power of attorney. Romans 3 [23]For all have sinned, and come short of the glory of God;

[24]Being justified freely by his grace through the redemption that is in Christ Jesus:

[25]Whom God hath set forth to be a propitiation through faith in his blood, to declare his righteousness for the remission of sins that are past, through the forbearance of God;

[26]To declare, I say, at this time his righteousness: that he might be just, and the justifier of him which believeth in Jesus.

Passing through this process we must work in victory, living as the children of God and honoring God by all manner of service; resisting all the works of the devil and taking back our rights that the thief steals.

Israel understood that the wealth they received in Egypt was for the purpose of service to the Lord. When they did, the favor of God dwelt among them—nobody got sick or suffered calamity. No enemy could stand before them. No mountain or hill could be a hindrance to Israel as long they remained faithful in the will of God.

They saw that God was their provider and their deliverer; He decided to show them his presence both day and night. When David understood that his fight was not his but God's, he did not spare any place for doubt or fear and he utilized insignificant tools to destroy Goliath. The stones he took were just a formality to humiliate a strong man and a strong nation by the anointing of the fresh oil to his stones.

Though Hannah knew that God made her barren, she took the step of faith turning to the supernatural to ask her right. And God gave her a master child who was incomparable among all the children of Elkanah.

1 Sam [4]And when the time was that Elkanah offered, he gave to Peninnah his wife, and to all her sons and her daughters, portions:

[5]But unto Hannah he gave a worthy portion; for he loved Hannah: but the LORD had shut up her womb. [10]And she was in bitterness of soul, and prayed unto the LORD, and wept sore.

¹¹And she vowed a vow, and said, O LORD of hosts, if thou wilt indeed look on the affliction of thine handmaid, and remember me, and not forget thine handmaid, but wilt give unto thine handmaid a man child, then I will give him unto the LORD all the days of his life, and there shall no razor come upon his head.

¹²And it came to pass, as she continued praying before the LORD, that Eli marked her mouth.

¹³Now Hannah, she spake in her heart; only her lips moved, but her voice was not heard: therefore Eli thought she had been drunken.

¹⁴And Eli said unto her, How long wilt thou be drunken? put away thy wine from thee.

¹⁵And Hannah answered and said, No, my lord, I am a woman of a sorrowful spirit: I have drunk neither wine nor strong drink, but have poured out my soul before the LORD.

¹⁶Count not thine handmaid for a daughter of Belial: for out of the abundance of my complaint and grief have I spoken hitherto.

¹⁷Then Eli answered and said, Go in peace: and the God of Israel grant thee thy petition that thou hast asked of him.

¹⁸And she said, Let thine handmaid find grace in thy sight. So the woman went her way, and did eat, and her countenance was no more sad.

¹⁹And they rose up in the morning early, and worshipped before the LORD, and returned, and came to their house to Ramah: and Elkanah knew Hannah his wife; and the LORD remembered her.

²⁰Wherefore it came to pass, when the time was come about after Hannah had conceived, that she bare a son,

and called his name Samuel, saying, Because I have asked him of the LORD.

²¹And the man Elkanah, and all his house, went up to offer unto the LORD the yearly sacrifice, and his vow.

The King Hezekiah received the message of his imminent death from God, he went to the supernatural to claim mercy and God gave him fifteen years more to his life.

2 Kings 20

¹In those days was Hezekiah sick unto death. And the prophet Isaiah the son of Amoz came to him, and said unto him, Thus saith the LORD, Set thine house in order; for thou shalt die and not live.

²Then he turned his face to the wall, and prayed unto the LORD, saying,

³I beseech thee, O LORD, remember now how I have walked before thee in truth and with a perfect heart, and have done that which is good in thy sight. And Hezekiah wept sore.

⁴And it came to pass, afore Isaiah was gone out into the middle court, that the word of the LORD came to him, saying,

⁵Turn again, and tell Hezekiah the captain of my people, Thus saith the LORD, the God of David thy father, I have heard thy prayer, I have seen thy tears: behold, I will heal thee: on the third day thou shalt go up unto the house of the LORD.

⁶And I will add unto thy days fifteen years; and I will deliver thee and this city out of the hand of the king of Assyria; and I will defend this city for mine own sake, and for my servant David's sake.

Sometimes people cry, "God visit us." But when God visits them, they do not know how to receive him, and the blessing can turn to a curse. When God visited Abraham and Sarah, they knew how to receive him and his angels. In contrast, the people of Sodom and Gomorrah were perverted; they wanted to know sexually the angels of God. Do you see the difference? Lot was vexed with the evil but was caught in the middle. The Bible tells us that those who receive the servants of God receive Jesus, and according to Matthew 10:40, there is a different reward for each ministry.

The Jews were praying day and night for the visitation of God but they did not understand the time and the process. When God descended in human form, they crucified him and the result was the Diaspora of the Jew and eventually the Jews were massacred in 70 AD. If you do not understand you cannot stand.

When the poor widow understood the process of receiving and respecting God's servant she invested all she had in the gospel and her life changed. When the rich man understood that his riches were nothing compared to the grace of God, he decided to climb a tree in order to see Jesus and he then allowed Jesus to transform his life.

Transformation and spiritual renewal and true revival came into his life. We must be transformed in our minds in order to touch and see signs and wonders. When you see anything from God, your first reaction must be to plant a seed, so you may benefit through his anointing and blessings; this is the system and the principle of God. The people who understand cannot constantly confess negativity in their lives. If they do, they may create a mess which will follow them everywhere. Do not be intimidated by someone who boasts to you of a lavish car or a building. You must stand in the presence of God uprightly, and God can make the owners of those companies come and expose their problems so you can pray for them. They will do this because they saw the power of God in you. The picture you see by faith, God will bring it to pass one day.

People have to stop with cold "religious" prayer and worship and enter deeply in spiritual adoration, banishing all vain words which reflect a lack of faith, knowing that without faith it is impossible to please God. Your holiness is hidden in your faith because in the true faith abide holiness and God's love; without faith there is no true holiness. If you are not receiving answers to prayer something must be wrong in the matter of faith. That is the reason the Word of God says, 'without faith it is impossible to please God.'

Your possession, your title and your position must kneel before God, not only your spirit. The way you think is what you are. Put the Word of God first; the promises of God are yours. Confess the Word in all circumstances and you will not be ashamed if you truly believe.

God didn't send anybody to destroy the sinners or the backsliders but to bring them to the light, using His love and compassion. We are not traveling with the names of backsliders but the name of Jesus. If I want to deal with such things, the Bible tells me to meet the person and talk with him, to show him the truth and pray for him and not to reject or to curse him. That is the mistake that many religious men do and it destroys not the devil, but the work of God.

Matthew 18

[11]For the Son of man is come to seek and to save that which was lost.

[15]Moreover if thy brother shall trespass against thee, go and tell him his fault between thee and him alone: if he shall hear thee, thou hast gained thy brother.

[16]But if he will not hear thee, then take with thee one or two more, that in the mouth of two or three witnesses every word may be established.

[17]And if he shall neglect to hear them, tell it unto the church: but if he neglect to hear the church, let him be unto thee as an heathen man and a publican.

1 John 5

[16]If any man see his brother sin a sin which is not unto death, he shall ask, and he shall give him life for them that sin not

unto death. There is a sin unto death: I do not say that he shall pray for it.

[17]All unrighteousness is sin: and there is a sin not unto death.

[18]We know that whosoever is born of God sinneth not; but he that is begotten of God keepeth himself, <u>and that wicked one toucheth him not.</u>

The past is past and God is not in the past. When he forgives he forgets; he doesn't need you to remind him of the sin of somebody or to condemn others. Keep your own heart pure and stop getting into other's business; it is not your task and it shall destroy you.

<u>John Bevere</u>

"We have seasons in life, God moves differently in each. We must discern the season, hear His word for the season, and move accordingly."

2

THE SUPERNATURAL REALITY IN ACTION

Jesus said that "we are not of the world." This means that we live in the natural but we have to live the supernatural by living the word that Jesus gave us. ALWAYS remember that the Lord gave to you and me the Word. That is our true wealth to enjoy and to use in different seasons. If the former apostles of Jesus were strong and Christlike it was because of that Word. This Word is still alive and powerful to the pulling down of the strongholds of the devil and to make free the captives.

> John 17; [14]I have given them thy word; and the world hath hated them, because they are not of the world, even as I am not of the world.

[15]I pray not that thou shouldest take them out of the world, but that thou shouldest keep them from the evil.

[16]They are not of the world, even as I am not of the world.

Romans 10: [8]But what saith it? The word is nigh thee, even in thy mouth, and in thy heart: that is, the word of faith, which we preach;

[9]That if thou shalt confess with thy mouth the Lord Jesus, and shalt believe in thine heart that God hath raised him from the dead, thou shalt be saved.

[10]For with the heart man believeth unto righteousness; and with the mouth confession is made unto salvation.

[11]For the scripture saith, Whosoever believeth on him shall not be ashamed.

This will happen when we surrender all to the leading of the Spirit through faith in God. Our way of dealing with things has to change; our ways of giving have to change and our entire mentality. When you are led by the Holy Spirit, the receiver has to be surprised and blessed because the Holy Spirit knows the real needs of everybody and all social concern. The anointing of God will escort our paths when we are led by the Holy Spirit. Victory is mine when I understand this reality. The children of God have to walk according to the will of God and not according to the routine and the emotion. Boldness is needed in the supernatural realm. Joshua lived the supernatural when he believed that everywhere he placed his feet it would become his possession and no enemy would stand before him. A mighty man stands before him with an open sword but Joshua, without a weapon, didn't fear to speak with him in boldness. Daniel lived the supernatural life in the presence of the lions and they didn't open their mouths to kill him. Shadrack, Meshack and Abednego stayed in the raging furnace and nothing ruined them. Esther lived the supernatural when she broke the law of the kingdom and brought salvation to God's people. We have to choose to live either naturally or supernaturally by believing.

Lincoln Mugo

Recently I was praying to God to intervene for me as I was feeling quite unwell for quite a while, yet I was still going on with my work but feeling nagged by it. God said to me, "Why do you keep asking and begging for healing? You have power and authority over your illness. Command it, rebuke it and it shall flee from you." I did just that and got well. If you are there and you suffer, that is the key to your health. Perhaps there are a few other unwelcome issues in my life that I should command to leave. I am looking into it.

Today the Christian world is divided by many beliefs: those who accept prosperity and those who condemn it, **but God is the giver of the prosperity**

Isaiah 45, 7. I form the light and create darkness, I bring prosperity and create disaster; I, the LORD, do all these things.

If you refuse to eat good food it is your problem but I need it. I believe God to give things that I need such as a new house, a vehicle with zero mileage, and so on. When I declare "prosperity is mine" there is no sin I do: if I confess that my family is blessed, my basket blessed, my future blessed and my dreams are to be fulfilled completely, it is for my advantage and God loves sons who live by faith. The way you think will become your identity and by this it will be determined if you are in the natural or the supernatural. No matter where you pass, the decision of your heart will put you into another dimension. No matter what sin you have committed, if you confess and repent and forsake the sin, God has forgiven you. No matter your failure, by transformation you will move into a new and good experience. We are winners and the instrument of war is God.

When we walk in the supernatural reality, miracles are evident and we do not struggle to get them. Healing is yours and you have divine protection. Your divine provision is guaranteed by God and not by another system. The culture of this supernatural world is faith and living the Word led by the Holy Spirit. The church needs the true transformation to grasp new reality in the supernatural realm. I am the child of God; I am an adopted son or daughter of God if the character of my Father resides in me. My Father is with me to fulfill every point and period He has inspired. The natural to God is the miracle for human beings, and walking with God is a flow of wonders, signs and miracles.

The Lord Jesus commanded Peter to walk in the supernatural; it worked when Peter obeyed the Word and started to walk on the water but when he thought about the culture of his nature he began to sink till he called for help to Jesus. Doubt in regard to the order of God is an enemy to our blessing and our promotion. I tell you that if Peter succeeded to obey that order he wouldn't need a ship to cross the river but the unbelief made him a loser.

Understanding your new nature will bring it into action easily in the supernatural; I do not have to force or to think but to believe and to do according to the new reality.

I am the living tabernacle of God and the Holy Spirit dwells in me, as long as I will respect this temple and yield permanently to God, no demon, no Satan, no fear and no doubt will stand before me. Fear shall fear me and doubt will tremble before me; then the manifestation of the Holy Spirit shall be permanent as the cloud of God dwells on the tabernacle in the wilderness.

This living tabernacle is protected by the strongest; in that way no power can resist or control the palace; but it shall continue to be invulnerable. We must avoid giving a space to unbelief and anything that grieves the Spirit. It means that, though the world rejects our ideas and persecutes us in many ways, we must not give a place to the devil. The strategy of the devil is to create hard and critical situations so trying that we come to curse God and ourselves. We have to be strong and stand, having all the weapons of God.

In the supernatural realm God controls and reigns; it is a great advantage to live supernatural realities. The world system cannot understand how miracles, wonders and signs follow us because the god of this world blinds their eyes. This is true indeed and we have to fulfill all the laws of the supernatural.

When I say that money shall look for me it depends on the seed I planted in the field of God. Desirable offerings make God happy and by that means the door of prosperity is open for me. As long as I will continue in righteousness and faith, God will do more and my situation will astonish people.

Yesterday and today are completely different, if I didn't succeed yesterday it doesn't mean that I shall stay there. The power of God and his direction shall make me different from the world system and I will enjoy the presence and the provision of God.

What if my seeds or offerings to God are like trash. I do not have anything worthy to confess my prosperity. We must plant good seeds that God shall multiply and bring us into another dimension of glory.

Before Elisha died, King Joash came to him seeking help against his enemies; when Elisha was in a supernatural reality, he told to the king to use his arrow and he only did so three times in II Kings 13: 18-19. Elisha told him that because he did not hit it five or six times he would beat his enemies only three times. It is possible to enter in the supernatural realm and plant the seed for seven elevations or promotions. It is possible for you to plant seven powerful seeds for it will never limit God. He can do far more than your expectation. Though Elisha had died, his bones resurrected a dead person who was thrown in his tomb.

All that God gives to us in the supernatural is not for our glory but for his glory, his honor, his magnificence and to bring sinners to repentance and to receive salvation.

The supernatural realm is for the children of God, using correctly the Word of God, assisted by the Holy Spirit of God.

Mary accepted the supernatural reality and she bore a son without the intervention of a man. Joshua stopped the earth by his word. Moses accomplished much by obeying, no matter what God told him.

THERE IS POWER INSIDE YOU; ACTIVATE IT TO YOUR SUCCESS. (The power inside you by Dr. RAHA MUGISHO)

A. God is the source and provider of real power.

Every man has been created with enough power inside him.

That is the reason God declared, "Let us create man in our image" Gen. 1:26.

He gave to him the power to subdue the earth and to be the leader of his creation.

Adam tested this power by giving names to animals and also to Eve.

God wanted Adam to exercise freely the power inside him.

Even today, God wants everybody to exercise this power in his life.

That is the reason for differences between one human and another.

Abel and Cain were two different men, sons of Adam, but each had his way to exploit the power inside him.

Abel exercised his power to make a good offering to God while his brother did the opposite. He gave to God cursed things (it means from the cursed earth)

God approved the product of Abel and rejected that of Cain.

Both were free to choose how to orient their power to their worship.

Their father gave them the word and left them to exercise their power.

The power may be used to build or to destroy. The Choice is up to you.

When we allow people to manifest their power, the freedom to decide should have a place. The freedom to choose and to do things.

When we do according to the will of someone, it is difficult to release our power. This is because we are working on the released power of somebody else.

What is the effectiveness of any meeting? It is when everybody expresses his idea freely without fear and pressure. In this way we will collect new information and different viewpoints, which will enrich our projects. Information is power. Do not neglect that point.

Charles Stanley says, "Until you give God total control of your life, there always will be a battle raging within your heart" (In Touch, March, 1995).

"My conscience is captive to the Word of God. Here I stand, I can do no other."—Martin Luther.

Galatians 6:7 "Do not be deceived, God is not mocked: for whatever a man sows, that he will reap." We are accountable for our choices, and consequences are a guarantee.

It is never easy to face the negative consequences when we struggle daily to live as God wants us too. You can choose to fix the old car rather than go into debt for a new car and make the wise decision that will ultimately return to you a sound financial standing. You have choices. The consequences you reap will be determined by the choices you make.

The consequences don't have to be negative. They can be positive, depending on whether you sow to your sinful nature or to the Holy Spirit.

Guard your heart and mind from things that would come between you and the truth.

The demons of TV and the computer send invitations to your credit card to make all kinds of false investments. Loans are not helpful at all times. These demons of loans come to destroy you and to enslave you all your life.

It is very important to renew your mind with the truth and it must be a daily habit. This must be a priority in our daily schedule. Renewing our minds with God's Word is the best practice to help us to avoid the unpleasant consequences of unwise decisions.

It is illogical to invest all of our time, energy, and skill just for money.

Paul reminds you not to do your work to be seen of men. You should do your work whether anyone is watching or not because you know God is watching. You should do your very best because the Holy Spirit is equipping and energizing you.

Don't let anybody make you believe that you are nobody.

God never created a nobody. He always does an excellent job.

Even if all your partners turn away, you have to encourage yourself in the Lord.

David, a man after the heart of God, passed many hard tests.

But one thing he never did was to remain backslidden or discouraged.

He knew how to encourage himself in the Lord.

When He was fired by the King Achish, returning home to Ziklag, He found that their houses were burned and their families taken in captivity.

He and his six hundred people cried till they were tired.

His own people said that they'd stone David to death.

David encouraged himself and consulted God who assured him a victory.

He knew how to convince his people and went with them to battle.

Because of his determination, activating the power that God gave him, they won the battle.

Be careful of tired people; they can be very dangerous.

They can get you killed; they are professionals in speaking negatively and gossiping.

Leave them behind you and go your way of success.

Davis had two hundred tired people; he left them and went with four hundred.

He understood that the battle is the Lord's, and God was with them.

By faith God gave them the desire of their hearts.

They delivered their families and took all their goods along with all they found in the Amalekite people's camp.

God is able to turn round the problem you have for his glory.

Sometimes God closes the familiar door of blessing to open a bigger one.

You may lose family, houses, and properties but God has always a way to give them back to you. Your hard time is a school that you passed and the promotion is on the way.

Strange situations can happen to you, not because you deserve it but by a divine purpose.

People always talk. Even in the time of Jesus, they criticized him.

They called him by many names but look today, we are living by his grace.

By his work on the cross we are justified; my sins and yours are deleted.

We are really free because the Son of God took all our offenses.

We are not guilty; we are holy by his holiness.

Powerful by His Power. Children of God by receiving and believing in Jesus.

King James Version (KJV)

1 Samuel 29

⁶Then Achish called David, and said unto him, Surely, as the LORD liveth, thou hast been upright, and thy going out and thy coming in with me in the host is good in my sight: for I have not found evil in thee since the day of thy coming unto me unto this day: nevertheless the lords favour thee not.

⁷Wherefore now return, and go in peace, that thou displease not the lords of the Philistines.

⁸And David said unto Achish, But what have I done? and what hast thou found in thy servant so long as I have been with thee unto this day, that I may not go fight against the enemies of my lord the king?

⁹And Achish answered and said to David, I know that thou art good in my sight, as an angel of God: notwithstanding the princes of the Philistines have said, He shall not go up with us to the battle.

¹⁰Wherefore now rise up early in the morning with thy master's servants that are come with thee: and as soon as ye be up early in the morning, and have light, depart.

¹¹So David and his men rose up early to depart in the morning, to return into the land of the Philistines. And the Philistines went up to Jezreel.

1 Samuel 30

¹And it came to pass, when David and his men were come to Ziklag on the third day, that the Amalekites had invaded the south, and Ziklag, and smitten Ziklag, and burned it with fire;

²And had taken the women captives that were therein: they slew not any, either great or small, but carried them away, and went on their way.

³So David and his men came to the city, and, behold, it was burned with fire; and their wives, and their sons, and their daughters, were taken captives.

⁴Then David and the people that were with him lifted up their voice and wept, until they had no more power to weep.

⁵And David's two wives were taken captives, Ahinoam the Jezreelitess, and Abigail the wife of Nabal the Carmelite.

⁶And David was greatly distressed; for the people spake of stoning him, because the soul of all the people was grieved, every man for his sons and for his daughters: but David encouraged himself in the LORD his God.

⁷And David said to Abiathar the priest, Ahimelech's son, I pray thee, bring me hither the ephod. And Abiathar brought thither the ephod to David.

⁸And David enquired at the LORD, saying, Shall I pursue after this troop? shall I overtake them? And he answered him, Pursue: for thou shalt surely overtake them, and without fail recover all.

⁹So David went, he and the six hundred men that were with him, and came to the brook Besor, where those that were left behind stayed.

¹⁰But David pursued, he and four hundred men: for two hundred abode behind, which were so faint that they could not go over the brook Besor.

¹⁷And David smote them from the twilight even unto the evening of the next day: and there escaped not a man of

them, save four hundred young men, which rode upon camels, and fled.

[18]And David recovered all that the Amalekites had carried away: and David rescued his two wives.

[19]And there was nothing lacking to them, neither small nor great, neither sons nor daughters, neither spoil, nor any thing that they had taken to them: David recovered all.

3

THE CONNECTION
IN THE SUPERNATURAL

No matter where you come from, no matter your race, no matter your education if you are connected to the Holy Ghost, miracles shall flow in your life. With this connection you will dwell in boldness of character and no space for fear and doubt will be in your habitation. Nobody can understand you unless he is in the same connection. When you fail in this connection you will start to act like Peter trying to walk on the water or Elijah running away from the face of Jezebel. Imagine a man who commanded the fire to descend and consume the army of Ahab—a man who just commanded fire to come down and burn the built altar. A man who prayed to stop the rain for three years and six months. How could he fear a woman? The answer is that he broke the connection and became like other men. The connection to God for Samson was to keep the covenant of uncut hair—without hair he became weak like all the weak.

John the Baptist had always great boldness when he was connected to God but when he began to think like the religious he got for a while a disconnection and sent people to ask who Jesus was.

There is a big difference between being connected to God and being connected to men of power or any influence. This is the reason many people connected to men of power fail and enter into confusion when they do not get what they expected to receive. But the strong connection to God empowers the subject and he or she becomes very strong in words and action.

It is very wise to look for the connection when something strange enters into your life and interferes with the Holy Spirit. We must rely on his power and his wisdom and not to tradition.

I can possess all my spiritual rights only when I stand in my new nature confessing the Word and declaring what belongs to me and resisting all the wiles of the enemies, chasing the Evil One off all my properties. I have the right to be healthy, to procreate, to have all kinds of material needs supplied. It is not in heaven where I will claim my rights. There everything is all right; there is no injustice.

Stay far from me, Satan. I cannot cooperate with you; I resist you in the name of Jesus. I transfer God's authority to my spiritual sons and daughters in Jesus' name. I believe in the provision of my Father and also in divine protection in Jesus' name.

2 Cor. 10

> [3]For though we walk in the flesh, we do not war after the flesh:
>
> [4](For the weapons of our warfare are not carnal, but mighty through God to the pulling down of strongholds;)

⁵Casting down imaginations, and every high thing that exalteth itself against the knowledge of God, and bringing into captivity every thought to the obedience of Christ;

⁶And having in a readiness to revenge all disobedience, when your obedience is fulfilled.

King James Version (KJV)

Psalm 23

¹The LORD is my shepherd; I shall not want.

²He maketh me to lie down in green pastures: he leadeth me beside the still waters.

³He restoreth my soul: he leadeth me in the paths of righteousness for his name's sake.

⁴Yea, though I walk through the valley of the shadow of death, I will fear no evil: for thou art with me; thy rod and thy staff they comfort me.

⁵Thou preparest a table before me in the presence of mine enemies: thou anointest my head with oil; my cup runneth over.

⁶Surely goodness and mercy shall follow me all the days of my life: and I will dwell in the house of the LORD forever.

This spoken word is very true as my bones are sound; there is no joke or comedy. God is my shepherd. He anointed my head with oil and my cup runs over; goodness and mercy shall follow me not only for one day but all the days of my life.

Praise God.

Better to create an atmosphere which will enable us to stay connected to the power of the Holy Spirit. This is the biblical way to live and to enter into the supernatural realm.

It is up to us to avoid any environments and actions which can withdraw us from the supernatural; be careful of people who are in the supernatural but on the other side. Do not be confused; they are connected to satanic power and they will have a bad end in their lives.

2 Corinthians 11

> [12]But what I do, that I will do, that I may cut off occasion from them which desire occasion; that wherein they glory, they may be found even as we.

> [13]For such are false apostles, deceitful workers, transforming themselves into the apostles of Christ.

> [14]And no marvel; for Satan himself is transformed into an angel of light.

> [15]Therefore it is no great thing if his ministers also be transformed as the ministers of righteousness; whose end shall be according to their works.

To whom you are connected is very important. If you are connected to the empty law of your religion, you will not make the devil tremble because he also has his religion. If you are connected to another source contrasting with Jesus' command, you are wasting your time and breath for nothing.

Sometimes you are connected but you miss the activation. You have to activate your connection by the words of God coming out of your mouth. When you are in good standing with God, Deuteronomy 28 is yours in the area of blessing and all the scriptures concerning your promotion or provision and protection are yours.

2009/09/23 20:12

Deuteronomy 28

New International Version (NIV)

Blessings for Obedience

¹If you fully obey the LORD your God and carefully follow all his commands I give you today, the LORD your God will set you high above all the nations on earth. ²All these blessings will come on you and accompany you if you obey the LORD your God:

³You will be blessed in the city and blessed in the country.

⁴The fruit of your womb will be blessed, and the crops of your land and the young of your livestock—the calves of your herds and the lambs of your flocks.

⁵Your basket and your kneading trough will be blessed.

⁶You will be blessed when you come in and blessed when you go out.

⁷The LORD will grant that the enemies who rise up against you will be defeated before you. They will come at you from one direction but flee from you in seven.

⁸The LORD will send a blessing on your barns and on everything you put your hand to. The LORD your God will bless you in the land he is giving you.

⁹The LORD will establish you as his holy people, as he promised you on oath, if you keep the commands of the LORD your God and walk in obedience to him. ¹⁰Then all the peoples on earth will see that you are called by the name of the LORD, and they will fear you. ¹¹The LORD will grant you abundant prosperity—in the fruit of your womb, the young of your livestock and the crops of your ground—in the land he swore to your ancestors to give you.

¹²The LORD will open the heavens, the storehouse of his bounty, to send rain on your land in season and to bless all the work of your hands. You will lend to many nations but will borrow from none. ¹³The LORD will make you the head, not the tail. If you pay attention to the commands of the LORD your God that I give you this day and carefully follow them, you will always be at the top, never at the bottom. ¹⁴Do not turn aside from any of the commands I give you today, to the right or to the left, following other gods and serving them.

By activating my connection, my daughter was raised from the dead and also another man of DRC. By activating my faith, money came into possession to pay my expenses. Many miracles happen in my ministry activating my connection. Without this activation I could be lost when people went against me in the time of weakness. But knowing that I had a true repentance, I didn't follow the voice of the devil but stayed connected to God, declaring my rights.

Any man in this world can fall into sin and be forgiven by repenting and when God forgives he forgets; he knows us better than any other person.

Psalm 103

[8]The LORD is merciful and gracious, slow to anger, and plenteous in mercy.

[9]He will not always chide: neither will he keep his anger forever.

[10]He hath not dealt with us after our sins; nor rewarded us according to our iniquities.

[11]For as the heaven is high above the earth, so great is his mercy toward them that fear him.

[12]As far as the east is from the west, so far hath he removed our transgressions from us.

[13]Like as a father pitieth his children, so the LORD pitieth them that fear him.

[14]For he knoweth our frame; he remembereth that we are dust.

The Lord knows our frame and it is because of his mercy that we succeed. Boldness is a great fruit in the supernatural realm. Once forgiven, go with your power to pull down all the strongholds of the devil.

This confession is good for you and better to confess it in time of trouble and weakness so you will update your force in the Lord. We are protected. We are more than conquerors. We are sons and daughters of God. We are his properties. We are the hammer of war and through us God will knock holes in the Enemy's lines for His glory.

I will praise The Lord who is my God.
The Lord is my redeemer.
He is my deliverer.
He is my hope.
He is the rock of my salvation.
The Lord purified me.
The Lord sanctified me.

The Lord is with me.

I dwell in His presence.

I have the divine protection.

He is my provider.

He is my source of joy.

He healed me totally.

He forgave all my sins.

He restores my soul.

His goodness and mercy shall escort me all the days of my life.

I shall not die but I shall live for the glory of God.

I am the living tabernacle of God and the cloud of the glory of God is upon me. God anointed me to preach the gospel, to heal the sick, to open the eyes of the blind. Miracles are mine, blessings are mine, healing is mine.

God opened a door of success to me that nobody can close.

God is the creator and the doer of wonders and signs.

Nothing is impossible to God. God is here; the glory of God is here.

God will never forget me.

God will give me more than seven elevations; seven blessings, seven promotions.

With my hand I will touch the goodness of God. With my eyes I shall see wonders and signs to my favor.

I am more than a conqueror; I am the hammer and instrument of war for God. I can do all things through God who strengthens me.

Heaven is mine, holiness is mine, and fresh anointing is mine. Money will follow me and God will multiply my seed.

Increase is mine, victory is mine.

I am in the presence of God; I am in the glory of God.

No weapon formed against me shall prosper. Jesus is the same yesterday, today and forever.

Boldness is mine, I believe in the supernatural and no devil will stand before me. God will give me a good end.

God will make all my projects to come true. Miracle, signs, wonders shall follow me.

God will make my name great and I always be above and
never beneath all the days of my life.

God will put me in a high position and my enemies will
come to kneel before my God. My seeds will come to
God and to me and no more family disappointments in
Jesus' name. I have the revelation of God and the Holy
Spirit is inside me.

PRAISE GOD. AMEN. I HAVE WON IN JESUS' NAME

Psalm 91

²I will say of the LORD, He is my refuge and my fortress:
my God; in him will I trust.

³Surely he shall deliver thee from the snare of the fowler, and
from the noisome pestilence.

⁴He shall cover thee with his feathers, and under his wings
shalt thou trust: his truth shall be thy shield and buckler.

⁵Thou shalt not be afraid for the terror by night; nor for the
arrow that flieth by day;

[6]Nor for the pestilence that walketh in darkness; nor for the destruction that wasteth at noonday.

[7]A thousand shall fall at thy side, and ten thousand at thy right hand; but it shall not come nigh thee.

[8]Only with thine eyes shalt thou behold and see the reward of the wicked.

[9]Because thou hast made the LORD, which is my refuge, even the most High, thy habitation;

[10]There shall no evil befall thee, neither shall any plague come nigh thy dwelling.

[11]For he shall give his angels charge over thee, to keep thee in all thy ways.

4

No Impossibility
In The Supernatural

I want to encourage the body of Christ in the truth. God will never be happy when we tell to this world that this and that are impossible. This is to attack God, doubting in his affirmative action. Even though I do not understand some situations, I have to keep on believing that nothing is impossible for God. We servants of God have to stand with boldness and confess together that nothing is impossible to God. No matter your problem, when you compare it face to face with the power of God, it is nothing. Beloved, it is time to take possession of our rights by resisting the devil in any area of your life. You will win. Trust me, it will work; nothing is impossible to God. I love you and I release the

31

power of God to touch your total being that you may grasp the reality of God and be comfortable in all your business.

> [7]Submit yourselves therefore to God. Resist the devil, and he will flee from you (James 4).

Power is mine, blessing is mine, holiness is mine. Surely by obeying the Word of God, I am the head and not the tail; I am healed by his stripes. I am lifted up by his glory. Praise God who prepares a table in the sight of my enemies, the devil is defeated and you and me—we have won.

Hebrews 11

> [1]Now faith is the substance of things hoped for, the evidence of things not seen.

> [2]For by it the elders obtained a good report.

> [3]Through faith we understand that the worlds were framed by the word of God, so that things which are seen were not made of things which do appear.

> [4]By faith Abel offered unto God a more excellent sacrifice than Cain, by which he obtained witness that he was righteous, God testifying of his gifts: and by it he being dead yet speaketh.

> [5]By faith Enoch was translated that he should not see death; and was not found, because God had translated him: for before his translation he had this testimony, that he pleased God.

> [6]But without faith it is impossible to please him: for he that cometh to God must believe that he is, and that he is a rewarder of them that diligently seek him.

> [7]By faith, Noah, being warned of God of things not seen as yet, moved with fear, prepared an ark to the saving of his

house; by the which he condemned the world, and became heir of the righteousness which is by faith.

⁸By faith, Abraham, when he was called to go out into a place which he should after receive for an inheritance, obeyed; and he went out, not knowing whither he went.

⁹By faith he sojourned in the land of promise, as in a strange country, dwelling in tabernacles with Isaac and Jacob, the heirs with him of the same promise:

¹⁰For he looked for a city which hath foundations, whose builder and maker is God.

¹¹Through faith also Sara herself received strength to conceive seed, and was delivered of a child when she was past age, because she judged him faithful who had promised.

¹²Therefore sprang there even of one, and him as good as dead, so many as the stars of the sky in multitude, and as the sand which is by the sea shore innumerable.

The problem is not your sickness but your faith in healing; your problem is not the poverty but your belief about the provision of God. My problem is not the mountain but how I speak to the mountain. The drought you may be experiencing is because you do not connect your total being to the power of the Holy Spirit. Many want to serve the Lord but refuse the power of God. God is and remains almighty.

I believe in your total recovery in the name of Jesus; I believe in your capacity to procreate in the name of Jesus; I believe in your elevation in the name of Jesus; I believe in your fresh anointing right now in the name of Jesus. I don't care what the devil did but I praise the Lord who destroys all the work of the devil. I was lost and now I am found by the power of God. My expectation is great in the Lord and I am right for believing God in tremendous signs and wonders. I will not die before I finish all I have inside me to lift up the name of Jesus.

Far from me be false teaching. Jesus is enough and his words are the medicine this world needs. All the powers you can see, if they do not have the background of the word of God, they are vain and subject to loss among the people of God. Beware of dogs and . . .

[2]Beware of dogs, beware of evil workers, beware of the concision. Philippians 3:2

5

DISCONNECTION AND DEACTIVATION IN THE SUPERNATURAL

God is not the author of disconnection or deactivation. We are the subject. What we refuse to believe by faith becomes the problem in the supernatural. When we lose the boldness, immediately we allow fear and doubt. My faith keeps all my possession and my belongings—spiritually, physically and materially. We are the reason for increase and for decrease. He must increase and we must decrease. I am connected when I walk by faith and declare the promises of God. It doesn't come through a simple declaration but by possessing them by faith. When we forget the power of God and his presence in us, the devil can usher in confusion, as he did to Eve and it becomes easy to be disconnected from the supernatural reality and to live simply by emotion and tradition.

The way I choose to live may bring the activation or deactivation in the supernatural. Many religious folks are disconnected and deactivated because they do not believe a miracle can happen in their lives; and because of that they make God a liar. Somebody may sin and remain connected if he repents and abandons his weakness but you may be disconnected because of your refusal to walk under the principles of God. The disconnection can be easily remedied but the deactivation can take longer because it involved a decision to take another life of tradition, rules, and religious ways instead of walking by faith and resisting the devil in all things. Judas was disconnected and deactivated till he went and committed suicide.

When the woman with the issue of blood heard about Jesus, she activated her faith to enter into the supernatural and she believed that her connection would come when she touched the garment of Jesus and when these two elements came together she received an instant healing (Mark 5; 25-34).

Bartimaus also heard about Jesus; he activated his faith by believing that when he met Jesus, no matter how serious his blindness, his eyes would be opened. He heard that Jesus was on his way and he began to cry to the healer till his connection became true and the Lord called him to receive his sight. Notice that he kept calling out to Jesus, though people told him to shut up. Praise God (Mark 10: 46).

Hard situations, sickness, and misunderstanding can provoke a disconnection, but the good news is that these situations are the good ground to experiment and to manifest the power of God. Be strong in the Lord and always stand in his promises. Ephesians 6; [10]Finally, my brethren, be strong in the Lord, and in the power of his might.

> [11]Put on the whole armour of God that ye may be able to stand against the wiles of the devil.

¹²For we wrestle not against flesh and blood, but against principalities, against powers, against the rulers of the darkness of this world, against spiritual wickedness in high places.

¹³Wherefore take unto you the whole armour of God, that ye may be able to withstand in the evil day, and having done all, to stand.

¹⁴Stand therefore, having your loins girt about with truth, and having on the breastplate of righteousness;

All God's heroes were abandoned yet they stood alone with God through fire, water, imprisonment and hardship. They never gave up in discouragement and rejected their belief. Look at Paul standing before kings and governors; David in Ziklag; Samson in Lehi; and many valiant worriers.

Don't delay to reconnect to the supernatural and do not allow the deactivation. You have to avoid the environment of unbelief and tradition and choose to spend your time with the true warriors in the Lord who defeat the devil at all times. Share your testimony with others rather than your lamentations and worries. Wear all the weapons of God and stand to fight the battle of faith so you may deliver the victims. You are not a victim; you are the victorious winner, confessing the name of the Lord both day and night.

6

PRAY THE ANSWER IN THE SUPERNATURAL

We remind God of what He promised and, because he is faithful, he shall perform his Word. Our declaration and our confessions will transform the natural to the supernatural based on the Word of God. Here we do not pray in an attitude of worry and defeat but in the victory of God and the Word of God.

I am more than a conqueror; the power of God will enable me to reach beyond my expectation. The angel of God's camp is within my compound protecting both me and all my belongings. I am blessed, though I may see the opposite, because I walk by faith and not by sight. God will give me the ability to fulfill all my dreams. I am what God says I am and my title is not based on what the people think but what God is planning for me. They will fight me but they will not win over me.

God will make my name great. Genesis 12 ²And I will make of thee a great nation, and I will bless thee, and make thy name great; and thou shalt be a blessing:

God said that whatsoever I do shall prosper. Psalm 1; ¹Blessed is the man that walketh not in the counsel of the ungodly, nor standeth in the way of sinners, nor sitteth in the seat of the scornful.

> ²But his delight is in the law of the LORD; and in his law
> doth he meditate day and night.

[3]And he shall be like a tree planted by the rivers of water, that bringeth forth his fruit in his season; his leaf also shall not wither; and whatsoever he doeth shall prosper.

God said I shall be always above and not beneath: Deuteronomy 28; [13]And the LORD shall make thee the head, and not the tail; and thou shalt be above only, and thou shalt not be beneath; if that thou hearken unto the commandments of the LORD thy God, which I command thee this day, to observe and to do them:

God said that He is my help and my refuge in time of trouble. Psalm 46 [1]God is our refuge and strength, a very present help in trouble.

[2]Therefore will not we fear, though the earth be removed, and though the mountains be carried into the midst of the sea;

God has my promotion in mind. Psalm75 [6]For promotion cometh neither from the east, nor from the west, nor from the south.

[7]But God is the judge: he putteth down one, and setteth up another

God said I have to remind or reason with him. Isaiah1; [18]Come now, and let us reason together, saith the LORD: though your sins be as scarlet, they shall be as white as snow; though they be red like crimson, they shall be as wool.

[19]If ye be willing and obedient, ye shall eat the good of the land:

God said He will protect me over water and over fire. Isaiah 43 [1]But now thus saith the LORD that created thee, O Jacob, and he that formed thee, O Israel, Fear not: for I have redeemed thee, I have called thee by thy name; thou art mine.

[2]When thou passest through the waters, I will be with thee; and through the rivers, they shall not overflow thee: when thou walkest through the fire, thou shalt not be burned; neither shall the flame kindle upon thee.

God said his word will not return void but shall accomplish his purpose. Isaiah 55 [8]For my thoughts are not your thoughts, neither are your ways my ways, saith the LORD.

[9]For as the heavens are higher than the earth, so are my ways higher than your ways, and my thoughts than your thoughts.

[10]For as the rain cometh down, and the snow from heaven, and returneth not thither, but watereth the earth, and maketh it bring forth and bud, that it may give seed to the sower, and bread to the eater:

[11]So shall my word be that goeth forth out of my mouth: it shall not return unto me void, but it shall accomplish that which I please, and it shall prosper in the thing whereto I sent it.

God said that no weapon formed against me shall prosper. Isaiah 54 [17]No weapon that is formed against thee shall prosper; and every tongue that shall rise against thee in judgment thou shalt condemn. This is the heritage of the servants of the LORD, and their righteousness is of me, saith the LORD.

God said that I shall not give him rest till He establish my justice. Isaiah 62 [5]For as a young man marrieth a virgin, so shall thy sons marry thee: and as the bridegroom rejoiceth over the bride, so shall thy God rejoice over thee.

[6]I have set watchmen upon thy walls, O Jerusalem, which shall never hold their peace day nor night: ye that make mention of the LORD, keep not silence,

[7]And give him no rest, till he establish, and till he make Jerusalem a praise in the earth.

[8]The LORD hath sworn by his right hand, and by the arm of his strength, Surely I will no more give thy corn to be meat for thine enemies; and the sons of the stranger shall not drink thy wine, for the which thou hast laboured:

God said He knew me while I was in the womb of my mother and He consecrated me, giving me an order to destroy the kingdom of the devil and to build and plant his kingdom. Jeremiah 1 [4]Then the word of the LORD came unto me, saying,

> [5]Before I formed thee in the belly I knew thee; and before thou camest forth out of the womb I sanctified thee, and I ordained thee a prophet unto the nations.

> [6]Then said I, Ah, Lord GOD! behold, I cannot speak: for I am a child.

> [7]But the LORD said unto me, Say not, I am a child: for thou shalt go to all that I shall send thee, and whatsoever I command thee thou shalt speak.

> [8]Be not afraid of their faces: for I am with thee to deliver thee, saith the LORD.

> [9]Then the LORD put forth his hand, and touched my mouth. And the LORD said unto me, Behold, I have put my words in thy mouth.

> [10]See, I have this day set thee over the nations and over the kingdoms, to root out, and to pull down, and to destroy, and to throw down, to build, and to plant.

God said they will fight me but they will not win over me; Jeremiah [19]And they shall fight against thee; but they shall not prevail against thee; for I am with thee, saith the LORD, to deliver thee.

God said He has the thought of peace to me; Jeremiah 29; [11]For I know the thoughts that I think toward you, saith the LORD, thoughts of peace, and not of evil, to give you an expected end.

> [12]Then shall ye call upon me, and ye shall go and pray unto me, and I will hearken unto you.

[13]And ye shall seek me, and find me, when ye shall search for me with all your heart.

[14]And I will be found of you, saith the LORD: and I will turn away your captivity, and I will gather you from all the nations, and from all the places whither I have driven you, saith the LORD; and I will bring you again into the place whence I caused you to be carried away captive.

Mark 16; [15]And he said unto them, Go ye into all the world, and preach the gospel to every creature.

[16]He that believeth and is baptized shall be saved; but he that believeth not shall be damned.

[17]And these signs shall follow them that believe; In my name shall they cast out devils; they shall speak with new tongues;

[18]They shall take up serpents; and if they drink any deadly thing, it shall not hurt them; they shall lay hands on the sick, and they shall recover.

God said He will not forsake me or forget me. Hebrews 13 [5]Let your conversation be without covetousness; and be content with such things as ye have: for he hath said, I will never leave thee, nor forsake thee.

[6]So that we may boldly say, The Lord is my helper, and I will not fear what man shall do unto me.

[7]Remember them which have the rule over you, who have spoken unto you the Word of God: whose faith follow, considering the end of their conversation.

[8]Jesus Christ the same yesterday, and today, and forever.

The Word of God says nothing is impossible to God. [37]For with God nothing shall be impossible.

God has already blessed me; no curse or witches can succeed against me. Number 24 ⁷And he took up his parable, and said, Balak the king of Moab hath brought me from Aram, out of the mountains of the east, saying, Come, curse me Jacob, and come, defy Israel.

⁸How shall I curse whom God hath not cursed? or how shall I defy whom the LORD hath not defied?

⁹For from the top of the rocks I see him, and from the hills I behold him: lo, the people shall dwell alone, and shall not be reckoned among the nations.

¹⁰Who can count the dust of Jacob, and the number of the fourth part of Israel? Let me die the death of the righteous, and let my last end be like his!

God is not a man to lie or a son of man to repent. Number 23 ¹⁹God is not a man, that he should lie; neither the son of man, that he should repent: hath he said, and shall he not do it? or hath he spoken, and shall he not make it good?

²⁰Behold, I have received commandment to bless: and he hath blessed; and I cannot reverse it.

²¹He hath not beheld iniquity in Jacob, neither hath he seen perverseness in Israel: the LORD his God is with him, and the shout of a king is among them.

²²God brought them out of Egypt; he hath as it were the strength of an unicorn.

²³Surely there is no enchantment against Jacob, neither is there any divination against Israel: according to this time it shall be said of Jacob and of Israel, What hath God wrought!

²⁴Behold, the people shall rise up as a great lion, and lift up himself as a young lion: he shall not lie down until he eat of the prey, and drink the blood of the slain.

God said I am his hammer and an instrument of war. Jeremiah 51 [20]Thou art my battle axe and weapons of war: for with thee will I break in pieces the nations, and with thee will I destroy kingdoms;

> [21]And with thee will I break in pieces the horse and his rider; and with thee will I break in pieces the chariot and his rider;

God said that the last glory of this house shall be greater than the first. Haggai 2 [5]According to the word that I covenanted with you when ye came out of Egypt, so my spirit remaineth among you: fear ye not.

> [6]For thus saith the LORD of hosts; Yet once, it is a little while, and I will shake the heavens, and the earth, and the sea, and the dry land;

> [7]And I will shake all nations, and the desire of all nations shall come: and I will fill this house with glory, saith the LORD of hosts.

> [8]The silver is mine, and the gold is mine, saith the LORD of hosts.

> [9]The glory of this latter house shall be greater than of the former, saith the LORD of hosts: and in this place will I give peace, saith the LORD of hosts.

God has anointed me. Luke 4 [17]And there was delivered unto him the book of the prophet Esaias. And when he had opened the book, he found the place where it was written,

> [18]The Spirit of the Lord is upon me, because he hath anointed me to preach the gospel to the poor; he hath sent me to heal the brokenhearted, to preach deliverance to the captives, and recovering of sight to the blind, to set at liberty them that are bruised,

> [19]To preach the acceptable year of the Lord.

God told me to ask him. Matt 7 ⁷Ask, and it shall be given you; seek, and ye shall find; knock, and it shall be opened unto you:

> ⁸For every one that asketh, receiveth; and he that seeketh, findeth; and to him that knocketh it shall be opened.

> ⁹Or what man is there of you, whom if his son ask bread, will he give him a stone?

> ¹⁰Or if he ask a fish, will he give him a serpent?

> ¹¹If ye then, being evil, know how to give good gifts unto your children, how much more shall your Father which is in heaven give good things to them that ask him?

> ¹²Therefore all things whatsoever ye would that men should do to you, do ye even so to them: for this is the law and the prophets.

God is pleased to release mercy. Matt 9 ¹²But when Jesus heard that, he said unto them, They that be whole need not a physician, but they that are sick.

> ¹³But go ye and learn what that meaneth, I will have mercy, and not sacrifice: for I am not come to call the righteous, but sinners to repentance.

God gave me the power to chase demons. Matt 10 ¹And when he had called unto him his twelve disciples, he gave them power against unclean spirits, to cast them out, and to heal all manner of sickness and all manner of disease. ⁷And as ye go, preach, saying, The kingdom of heaven is at hand.

> ⁸Heal the sick, cleanse the lepers, raise the dead, cast out devils: freely ye have received, freely give.

God said whoever receive me he received Him and he shall have a reward. Matthew 10 ⁴⁰He that receiveth you receiveth me, and he that receiveth me receiveth him that sent me.

⁴¹He that receiveth a prophet in the name of a prophet shall receive a prophet's reward; and he that receiveth a righteous man in the name of a righteous man shall receive a righteous man's reward.

⁴²And whosoever shall give to drink unto one of these little ones a cup of cold water only in the name of a disciple, verily I say unto you, he shall in no wise lose his reward.

God said that his kingdom is for those who desire it violently. Matt 11 ¹²And from the days of John the Baptist until now the kingdom of heaven suffereth violence, and the violent take it by force.

God said if I believe nothing shall be impossible to me. Matt 17 ¹⁹Then came the disciples to Jesus apart, and said, Why could not we cast him out?

²⁰And Jesus said unto them, Because of your unbelief: for verily I say unto you, If ye have faith as a grain of mustard seed, ye shall say unto this mountain, Remove hence to yonder place; and it shall remove; and nothing shall be impossible unto you.

²¹Howbeit this kind goeth not out but by prayer and fasting.

God gave me the power to march on the scorpion and to all the power of the devil and nothing shall harm me. Luke 10 ¹⁸And he said unto them, I beheld Satan as lightning fall from heaven.

¹⁹Behold, I give unto you power to tread on serpents and scorpions, and over all the power of the enemy: and nothing shall by any means hurt you.

Today you are between two things that you must choose; either you accept these promises of God and enter into the supernatural or you stay in the tradition. I and my disciples choose to dwell in the supernatural, believing all the words of God. The transformation very deeply will occur in every area of your life if you accept the opportunity to change and swallow all these promises of God. God doesn't make discrimination of race, gender, color, education, size, title but He escorts his words. He is behind his words. He is the word.

The Word of God challenges me to be able to do all things having the power of God. Philippians 4:[13]I can do all things through Christ which strengtheneth me.

7

WISDOM IN THE
SUPERNATURAL REALITY

Better to know to distinguish what belongs to the Spirit, and what is the common act of a human being. No matter what your environment, you have to plant the seed of the Word coming out of your mouth; do not imitate profanity in all manners. Profanity is like an insult to the people you are supposed to impact with the life of Christ. Bad environments shall withdraw the connection and you will become like them. In all circumstances we have to know that we are a peculiar people, a royal priesthood.

1 Peter 2

⁹But ye are a chosen generation, a royal priesthood, an holy nation, a peculiar people; that ye should shew forth the praises of him who hath called you out of darkness into his marvellous light;

¹⁰Which in time past were not a people, but are now the people of God: which had not obtained mercy, but now have obtained mercy.

¹¹Dearly beloved, I beseech you as strangers and pilgrims, abstain from fleshly lusts, which war against the soul;

¹²Having your conversation honest among the Gentiles: that, whereas they speak against you as evildoers, they may by your good works, which they shall behold, glorify God in the day of visitation.

Our behavior and character must reflect the glory of God in words and deeds. We shall make a difference and they will come to us to seek for help.

Wherever you see God in anybody, be ready to sow a seed; there shall be a reward for this. Sow every time you have the possibility. God is the one who multiplies the seeds. ⁴He that observeth the wind shall not sow; and he that regardeth the clouds shall not reap.

⁵As thou knowest not what is the way of the spirit, nor how the bones do grow in the womb of her that is with child: even so thou knowest not the works of God who maketh all.

⁶In the morning sow thy seed, and in the evening withhold not thine hand: for thou knowest not whether shall prosper, either this or that, or whether they both shall be alike good.

We have to choose to do all things according the Word of God. As our faith controls all our being, the activation to the supernatural requires patience in faith, obedience by faith, great expectation by faith. It will not be an overnight process but it is creating a reality, a demonstration of the unseen brought to visibility. In time of trouble do not see the trouble but say a word against it. In time of sickness confess the word, giving you your right to healing; in time of lack confess a word concerning the multiplication by God to the seeds you planted. Never forget to pay your tithe and to plant your seeds at anytime, led by the Holy Spirit. Do not create a door of evil into your life. Your tongue may be the source of your success or your defeat.

James 3 ²For in many things we offend all. If any man offend not in word, the same is a perfect man, and able also to bridle the whole body.

> ³Behold, we put bits in the horses' mouths, that they may obey us; and we turn about their whole body.

> ⁴Behold also the ships, which though they be so great, and are driven of fierce winds, yet are they turned about with a very small helm, whithersoever the governor listeth.

> ⁵Even so the tongue is a little member, and boasteth great things. Behold, how great a matter a little fire kindleth!

> ⁶And the tongue is a fire, a world of iniquity: so is the tongue among our members, that it defileth the whole body, and setteth on fire the course of nature; and it is set on fire of hell.

> ⁷For every kind of beasts, and of birds, and of serpents, and of things in the sea, is tamed, and hath been tamed of mankind:

> ⁸But the tongue can no man tame; it is an unruly evil, full of deadly poison.

We must know what to say on different occasions and to be the doer of the word, for faith without works is dead. James 1; ¹⁷Even so faith, if it hath not works, is dead, being alone.

[18]Yea, a man may say, Thou hast faith, and I have works: shew me thy faith without thy works, and I will shew thee my faith by my works.

[19]Thou believest that there is one God; thou doest well: the devils also believe, and tremble.

[20]But wilt thou know, O vain man, that faith without works is dead?

[21]Was not Abraham our father justified by works, when he had offered Isaac his son upon the altar?

[22]Seest thou how faith wrought with his works, and by works was faith made perfect?

[23]And the scripture was fulfilled which saith, Abraham believed God, and it was imputed unto him for righteousness: and he was called the Friend of God.

[24]Ye see then how that by works a man is justified, and not by faith only.

[25]Likewise also was not Rahab the harlot justified by works, when she had received the messengers, and had sent them out another way?

[26]For as the body without the spirit is dead, so faith without works is dead also.

Do not curse your life or your future. Instead, keep silent when you do not have an appropriate word to say. Give by faith, forgive by faith, love by faith, walk by faith; do not give any place to the devil. All these are for your advantage; do not allow your mouth to gossip, this will defile you. When you allow your eyes to see sexual immorality or to hear profanity, you will get a disconnection in the supernatural and you will become subject to distraction and confusion. Always remember that we are a chosen race, a holy nation, a peculiar people and a royal priesthood.

Do not be the slave of your words, repent and correct them. The situation you see is not permanent. It will pass to your favor when you speak an appointed word to it. Know that all things work together for our good. Do not give up, by faith you will be on the top and not beneath.

Roman 8 ²⁸And we know that all things work together for good to them that love God, to them who are the called according to his purpose.

The season will change in your favor. God shall bring an opportunity to save you from the deep hole that the devil has created to harm you; remember that no weapon of the enemies shall prosper against you. You will be above and protected. Alleluia, we are protected, we are lifted, and we are kings, queens, prince and princesses, a royal priesthood.

David was forgotten by all the members of his family but not God. When he faced lions, he didn't look for any help but the power of God; without his belief in the supernatural he would have been killed by the lion and also by Goliath but, praise the Lord, God did not forsake him. He made his name great. God will give you a name greater than the heir of your family. He will always promote you as long you dwell in his principles, declaring his words instead of empty tradition and unbelief.

Never mind, though the season seems long, the harvest shall come and we will enjoy the blessing of God. Do not give up, expect a miracle. God can never be late. He is coming at a good and appropriate time to reward us.

You will have what you say, so pay attention to each word out of your mouth. The Bible has taught us the power of our confessions and our belief in our hearts; it is true indeed that people confess the faith they have in their hearts.

Romans 10 ⁸But what saith it? The word is nigh thee, even in thy mouth, and in thy heart: that is, the word of faith, which we preach;

⁹That if thou shalt confess with thy mouth the Lord Jesus, and shalt believe in thine heart that God hath raised him from the dead, thou shalt be saved.

¹⁰For with the heart man believeth unto righteousness; and with the mouth confession is made unto salvation.

¹¹For the scripture saith, Whosoever believeth on him shall not be ashamed.

The picture you see by faith shall come to pass by the power of God. Do not neglect your destiny. God created you to succeed, do not seek everyone to approve you; it is already done by God himself and not a man. Know that humans change but God never changes. Who told you that you are barren? Who told you that you are poor? Who told you that you are useless? Who told you that you will die before achieving your life goals? The answer is not God but the wiles of Satan that threaten to destroy your future and your destiny. Resist Satan with all your faith and tell him, "Not me, you father of lies. I am more than a conqueror. My God will give me the desire of my heart." Keep on confessing the promise of God to your situation and, believe me, it shall work. As I am alive and the Word of God is with me, do not hesitate to meet me personally if you need extra help from God. I am your servant sent by God, I am your brother in Christ and I love you. Receive your healing right now in Jesus' name. Be anointed right now in Jesus' name. Be delivered in the name of Jesus. May God visit your activities and touch them for your elevation right now in Jesus' name. Believe and receive in the name of Jesus.

8

MIRACLES OCCUR ALWAYS BY BOLDNESS OF FAITH AND NOT BY EMOTION

Jacob, Moses, Joshua, Elijah, Elisha, Jesus, the Apostles of Jesus, the various servants of God . . .

All these people received miracles by the spoken word and not by emotion. They knew their God and were connected to the higher power without doubt and fear. They proved their difference by faith, transforming the natural to the supernatural. They did the will of God. They knew it and they knew that they were the true servants of God.

Jacob had the vision of prosperity from the sheep of his father-in-law. He spoke what he wanted and performed an act of faith. Then he became rich and powerful because God was with him and he knew how to gain spiritual advantage.

Genesis 30

³¹And he said, What shall I give thee? And Jacob said, Thou shalt not give me any thing: if thou wilt do this thing for me, I will again feed and keep thy flock.

³²I will pass through all thy flock to day, removing from thence all the speckled and spotted cattle, and all the brown cattle among the sheep, and the spotted and speckled among the goats: and of such shall be my hire.

³³So shall my righteousness answer for me in time to come, when it shall come for my hire before thy face: every one that is not speckled and spotted among the goats, and brown among the sheep, that shall be counted stolen with me.

³⁴And Laban said, Behold, I would it might be according to thy word.

³⁵And he removed that day the he goats that were ringstraked and spotted, and all the she goats that were speckled and spotted, and every one that had some white in it, and all the brown among the sheep, and gave them into the hand of his sons.

³⁶And he set three days' journey betwixt himself and Jacob: and Jacob fed the rest of Laban's flocks.

³⁷And Jacob took him rods of green poplar, and of the hazel and chesnut tree; and pilled white strakes in them, and made the white appear which was in the rods.

³⁸And he set the rods which he had pilled before the flocks in the gutters in the watering troughs when the flocks came to drink, that they should conceive when they came to drink.

³⁹And the flocks conceived before the rods, and brought forth cattle ringstraked, speckled, and spotted.

⁴⁰And Jacob did separate the lambs, and set the faces of the flocks toward the ringstraked, and all the brown in the flock of Laban; and he put his own flocks by themselves, and put them not unto Laban's cattle.

⁴¹And it came to pass, whensoever the stronger cattle did conceive, that Jacob laid the rods before the eyes of the cattle in the gutters that they might conceive among the rods.

⁴²But when the cattle were feeble, he put them not in: so the feebler were Laban's, and the stronger Jacob's.

⁴³And the man increased exceedingly, and had much cattle, and maidservants, and menservants, and camels, and asses.

Moses declared miracle words to Pharaoh and several miracles happened in Egypt till they got the deliverance. He divided by the power of God the Red Sea. He received miracles of food, water and his adversaries were punished in a strange way.

Exodus 9

²⁹And Moses said unto him, As soon as I am gone out of the city, I will spread abroad my hands unto the LORD; and the thunder shall cease, neither shall there be any more hail; that thou mayest know how that the earth is the LORD's.

³³And Moses went out of the city from Pharaoh, and spread abroad his hands unto the LORD: and the thunders and hail ceased, and the rain was not poured upon the earth.

³⁴And when Pharaoh saw that the rain and the hail and the thunders were ceased, he sinned yet more, and hardened his heart, he and his servants.

Exodus 11

¹And the LORD said unto Moses, Yet will I bring one plague more upon Pharaoh, and upon Egypt; afterwards he will let you go hence: when he shall let you go, he shall surely thrust you out hence altogether.

²Speak now in the ears of the people, and let every man borrow of his neighbour, and every woman of her neighbour, jewels of silver and jewels of gold.

³And the LORD gave the people favour in the sight of the Egyptians. Moreover the man Moses was very great in the land of Egypt, in the sight of Pharaoh's servants, and in the sight of the people.

⁴And Moses said, Thus saith the LORD, About midnight will I go out into the midst of Egypt:

⁵And all the firstborn in the land of Egypt shall die, from the first born of Pharaoh that sitteth upon his throne, even unto the firstborn of the maidservant that is behind the mill; and all the firstborn of beasts.

⁶And there shall be a great cry throughout all the land of Egypt, such as there was none like it, nor shall be like it any more.

⁷But against any of the children of Israel shall not a dog move his tongue, against man or beast: that ye may know how that the LORD doth put a difference between the Egyptians and Israel.

⁸And all these thy servants shall come down unto me, and bow down themselves unto me, saying, Get thee out, and

all the people that follow thee: and after that I will go out. And he went out from Pharaoh in a great anger. Exodus 14; [13]And Moses said unto the people, Fear ye not, stand still, and see the salvation of the LORD, which he will shew to you today: for the Egyptians whom ye have seen today, ye shall see them again no more forever.

[14]The LORD shall fight for you, and ye shall hold your peace.

[15]And the LORD said unto Moses, Wherefore criest thou unto me? speak unto the children of Israel, that they go forward:

[16]But lift thou up thy rod, and stretch out thine hand over the sea, and divide it: and the children of Israel shall go on dry ground through the midst of the sea.

[17]And I, behold, I will harden the hearts of the Egyptians, and they shall follow them: and I will get me honour upon Pharaoh, and upon all his host, upon his chariots, and upon his horsemen.

[18]And the Egyptians shall know that I am the LORD, when I have gotten me honour upon Pharaoh, upon his chariots, and upon his horsemen.

[19]And the angel of God, which went before the camp of Israel, removed and went behind them; and the pillar of the cloud went from before their face, and stood behind them:

[20]And it came between the camp of the Egyptians and the camp of Israel; and it was a cloud and darkness to them, but it gave light by night to these: so that the one came not near the other all the night.

[21]And Moses stretched out his hand over the sea; and the LORD caused the sea to go back by a strong east wind

all that night, and made the sea dry land, and the waters were divided.

²²And the children of Israel went into the midst of the sea upon the dry ground: and the waters were a wall unto them on their right hand, and on their left.

²³And the Egyptians pursued, and went in after them to the midst of the sea, even all Pharaoh's horses, his chariots, and his horsemen.

²⁴And it came to pass, that in the morning watch the LORD looked unto the host of the Egyptians through the pillar of fire and of the cloud, and troubled the host of the Egyptians,

²⁵And took off their chariot wheels, that they drave them heavily: so that the Egyptians said, Let us flee from the face of Israel; for the LORD fighteth for them against the Egyptians.

²⁶And the LORD said unto Moses, Stretch out thine hand over the sea, that the waters may come again upon the Egyptians, upon their chariots, and upon their horsemen.

²⁷And Moses stretched forth his hand over the sea, and the sea returned to his strength when the morning appeared; and the Egyptians fled against it; and the LORD overthrew the Egyptians in the midst of the sea.

²⁸And the waters returned, and covered the chariots, and the horsemen, and all the host of Pharaoh that came into the sea after them; there remained not so much as one of them.

²⁹But the children of Israel walked upon dry land in the midst of the sea; and the waters were a wall unto them on their right hand, and on their left.

³⁰Thus the LORD saved Israel that day out of the hand of the Egyptians; and Israel saw the Egyptians dead upon the sea shore.

³¹And Israel saw that great work which the LORD did upon the Egyptians: and the people feared the LORD, and believed the LORD, and his servant Moses.

Elijah, by his spoken word, closed heaven from receiving rain three years and six months. By his word the rain came the same day he promised to Ahab.

The miracle of oil and flour increased by his spoken word to the widow and it came to pass. The river Jordan was divided in his presence and he passed on the dry way. By his spoken word fire descended and consumed officers sent to arrest him. By his boldness he showed to Israel before the false prophet of Jezebel that Jehovah is the true God. He was the second person to be caught up because he succeeded in all the principles of the supernatural.

1 Kings

¹³And Elijah said unto her, Fear not; go and do as thou hast said: but make me thereof a little cake first, and bring it unto me, and after make for thee and for thy son.

¹⁴For thus saith the LORD God of Israel, The barrel of meal shall not waste, neither shall the cruse of oil fail, until the day that the LORD sendeth rain upon the earth.

¹⁵And she went and did according to the saying of Elijah: and she, and he, and her house, did eat many days.

¹⁶And the barrel of meal wasted not, neither did the cruse of oil fail, according to the word of the LORD, which he spake by Elijah.

¹⁷And it came to pass after these things, that the son of the woman, the mistress of the house, fell sick; and his sickness

was so sore, that there was no breath left in him. [18]And she said unto Elijah, What have I to do with thee, O thou man of God? art thou come unto me to call my sin to remembrance, and to slay my son?

[19]And he said unto her, Give me thy son. And he took him out of her bosom, and carried him up into a loft, where he abode, and laid him upon his own bed.

[20]And he cried unto the LORD, and said, O LORD my God, hast thou also brought evil upon the widow with whom I sojourn, by slaying her son?

[21]And he stretched himself upon the child three times, and cried unto the LORD, and said, O LORD my God, I pray thee, let this child's soul come into him again.

[22]And the LORD heard the voice of Elijah; and the soul of the child came into him again, and he revived.

[23]And Elijah took the child, and brought him down out of the chamber into the house, and delivered him unto his mother: and Elijah said, See, thy son liveth.

[24]And the woman said to Elijah, Now by this I know that thou art a man of God, and that the word of the LORD in thy mouth is truth.

The spoken word will bring miracles wherever we will be. Elisha by his words blessed, cursed, transformed situations, raised the dead, brought also the miracle of oil's increase to a widow whose sons were about to be sold because of the debt of her husband. Speak the word of faith instead of pleading and murmuring. We have the authority to speak and God will fulfill the spoken word of his servant.

Our Lord Jesus spoke to many situations and transformed the natural to the supernatural. He spoke to the wind, to death, he cursed the fig tree, commanded the unclean spirits to leave the bodies of people. He walked on the water and commanded Peter to walk too. He did the miracle of increase of fish and bread. Everywhere He spoke the word, the transformation came by wonders and miracles.

The apostles did the same: healing, resurrecting the dead, the cripples walked, the blind recovered their sight, the dumb spoke, the demons were cast out by the name of Jesus and the gospel was preached by signs and wonders. This is the full gospel. The Lord promised to fulfill his words by signs and wonders.

Mark 16

¹⁵And he said unto them, Go ye into the entire world, and preach the gospel to every creature.

¹⁶He that believeth and is baptized shall be saved; but he that believeth not shall be damned.

¹⁷And these signs shall follow them that believe; In my name shall they cast out devils; they shall speak with new tongues;

¹⁸They shall take up serpents; and if they drink any deadly thing, it shall not hurt them; they shall lay hands on the sick, and they shall recover.

¹⁹So then after the Lord had spoken unto them, he was received up into heaven, and sat on the right hand of God.

²⁰And they went forth, and preached everywhere, the Lord working with them, and confirming the word with signs following. Amen.

The gospel shall be confirmed with signs; this is the promise of the Lord.

Beyond healing and increase, God does tremendous things and nothing is impossible to God.

Smith Wigglesworth's Miracles

*Smith Wigglesworth, often referred to as 'the Apostle of Faith,'
was one of the pioneers of the Pentecostal revival that occurred
a century ago. Without human refinement and education he
was able to tap into the infinite resources of God to bring divine
grace to multitudes. Thousands came to Christian faith in his
meetings, hundreds were healed of serious illnesses and diseases
as supernatural signs followed his ministry. A deep intimacy
with his heavenly Father and an unquestioning faith in God's
Word brought spectacular results and provided an example for
all true believers of the Gospel.*

He wrote, ". . . I was able to devote much of my time to the sick and
needy. I used to go to Leeds every week to a place where Divine Healing
was taught. But I was very critical in my spirit and would judge people
so harshly. I did not know why so many people who taught Divine
Healing wore glasses. I questioned, "Why do you wear glasses if you
believe in Divine Healing?" This stumbled me somewhat. Later I had
to wear glasses to read my Bible, and I was often criticised for this.
However, I was very full of compassion toward the sick and needy folk,
and being able to pay the expenses of the needy ones, I used to collect
a number of them and take them to Leeds every Tuesday to the service.
One day I had nine with me. The leaders of the Leeds Healing Home
looked through the window and said, "Here is Wigglesworth coming
again and bringing a lot more. If he only knew, he could get these people
healed at Bradford just as easily as to get them healed in Leeds."

These leaders knew that I had a compassion for the sick and needy, and
one day they said to me: "We want to go to the Keswick convention
and we have been thinking whom we should leave to do the work. We
can only think of you." I said, "I couldn't conduct a healing service."
They said, "We have no one else. We trust you to take care of the work
while we are away." A flash came into my mind: "Well, any number
of people can talk. All I have to do is to take charge." The following
week when I got there, the place was full of people. Of course, the
first thing I did was to look for someone who would do the speaking;
but all whom I asked said, "No, you have been chosen and you must
do it." And so I had to begin. I do not remember what I said but I do

know that when I had finished speaking fifteen people came out for healing. One of these was a man from Scotland who hobbled on a pair of crutches. I prayed for him and he was instantly healed. There was no one so surprised as I was. He was jumping all over the place without his crutches. This encouraged the others to believe God for their healing and all the people were healed. I am sure it was not my faith, but it was God in His compassion coming to help me in that hour of need.

Smith in classic preaching pose, Bible at the ready!

After this the Lord opened the door of faith for me more and more. I announced that I would have a Divine Healing meeting in Bradford on a certain evening. I can remember that there were twelve people who came that night and all of those twelve were miraculously healed. One had a tongue badly bitten in the centre through a fall. This one was perfectly healed. Another was a woman with an ulcer on her ankle joint and a large sore that was constantly discharging. She was healed and there was only a scar the next day. The others were healed the same way.

One day a man asked me, "Does Divine Healing embrace seasickness?" I answered, "Yes. It is a spirit of fear that causes your seasickness, and I command that spirit to go out of you in Jesus' name." He was never seasick again though he had to travel much.

One day a man came to the house. He was a very devoted brother. I said to him, "Mr. Clark, you seem downcast today. What's up?" He answered, "I left my wife dying. Two doctors have been with her right through the night and they say she cannot live long." I said to him, "Why don't you believe God for your wife?" He answered, "Brother Wigglesworth, I cannot believe for her."

He went out of the house brokenhearted. I went to see a fellow named Howe who was opening a small mission in Bradford. I thought he was the right man to go with me to assist me. When I said, "Will you go with me?" he answered, "No, indeed I won't. Please do not ask me again. But I believe if you will go, God will heal." I realise now that the Lord put those words in his mouth to encourage me.

Well, I knew a man named Nichols who, if he got the opportunity to pray, would pray all around the world three times and then come back. So I went to him and said, "Will you come with me to pray for Sister Clark?" He answered, "Yes, I will be very glad." We had a mile and a half to walk to that house. I told him when he began to pray not to stop until he was finished. When we got to the house we saw that Mrs. Clark was nearly gone. I said to the one I had brought with me, "You see the dangerous condition of Sister Clark. Now don't waste time but begin to pray." Seeing he had an opportunity, he began. I had never suffered so much as I did when he was praying, and I cried to the Lord, "Stop him! Please, Lord, stop this man's praying." Why? Because he prayed for the dear husband who was going to be bereaved and for the children who were going to be motherless. He piled it on so thick that I had to cry out, "Stop him, Lord; I cannot stand this." And thank God, he stopped.

Though I knew that neither Clark nor Nichols believed in Divine Healing, I had concealed a small bottle in my hip pocket that would hold about half a pint of oil. I put a long cork in it so that I could open the bottle easily. I took the bottle out of my pocket and held it behind me, and said: "Now you pray, Mr. Clark." Brother Clark, being encouraged by Brother Nichols' prayer, prayed also that he might be sustained in his great bereavement. I could not stand it at all, and I cried, "Lord, stop him." I was so earnest and so broken that they could hear me outside the house. Thank God, he stopped.

As soon as he stopped, I pulled the cork out of the bottle, and went over to the dying woman who was laid out on the bed. I was a novice at this time and did not know any better, so I poured all the contents of that bottle of oil over Mrs. Clark's body in the name of Jesus!

I was standing beside her at the top of the bed and looking towards the foot, when suddenly the Lord Jesus appeared. I had my eyes open gazing at Him. There He was at the foot of the bed. He gave me one of those gentle smiles. I see Him just now as I tell this story to you. I have never lost that vision, the vision of that beautiful soft smile. After a few moments He vanished but something happened that day that changed my whole life. Mrs. Clark was raised up and filled with life, and lived to bring up a number of children; she outlived her husband many years.

Everybody has to have testings. If you believe in Divine Healing you will surely be tested on the faith line. God cannot bring anyone into blessing and into full co-operation with Him except through testings and trials.

TRANSFORMING WATER INTO PETROL

The example and miracles of Smith Wigglesworth inspire us to attain Ever Increasing Faith, by following Christ as he did. When you read transcripts of his sermons, you will find they carry the same anointing as when first spoken, and the Lord still works healing miracles through them **today**.

Here's an account of another miracle wrought by Smith's faith in Christ; not of healing, but of a very practical nature: Transforming water into petrol.

Turning water into petrol is the modern equivalent of the alchemist's dream of changing earth into gold. It's scientifically impossible, of course, but that doesn't stop crooks and tricksters from regularly 'discovering the secret'.

Recently, an Indian claimed to be able to change water into petrol, and convincingly demonstrated the feat in public. His aim was to obtain a lucrative contract with substantial down payment for the secrets of the process. No doubt, swiftly followed by a vanishing act.

This was his pitch: Genuine water was volunteered and tasted by onlookers to prove it was pure, he poured the water into a glass beaker, and heated it to boiling. Then stirring with a glass rod, accompanied by ad lib hocus-pocus, he removed it from the heat source, and invited experts to examine the product of his labours.

Indeed it smelt like petrol, and when a lighted match was dropped in, the beaker burst into flames, to the delight of everyone watching.

You've no doubt guessed the trick already. His glass rod was hollow, filled with petrol, and sealed at the tip with a plug of wax. When he stirred the boiling water, the wax melted, released the petrol, which floated on the water, and convinced the sceptics.

That is Satan's work; deception, fraud, and trickery. God's way is altogether different.

The things which are impossible with men **are possible with God.**
Holy Bible, Lk. 18:27, KJV

When I was in the plumbing business I enjoyed praying for the sick. Urgent calls would come and I would have no time to wash, and with my hands all black I would preach to these sick ones, my heart all aglow with love. Ah, you must have your heart in the thing when you pray for the sick. You have to get right to the bottom of the cancer with a divine compassion and then you will see the gifts of the Spirit in operation.

I was called at 10 o'clock one night to pray for a young person given up by the doctor who was dying of consumption. As I looked, I saw that unless God undertook it was impossible for her to live. I turned to the mother and said, "Well, mother, you will have to go to bed." She said, "Oh, I have not had my clothes off for three weeks." I said to the daughters, "You will have to go to bed," but they did not want to go. It was the same with the son. I put on my overcoat and said, "Good-bye, I'm off." They said, "Oh, don't leave us." I said, "I can do nothing here." They said, "Oh, if you will stop, we will all go to bed." I knew that God would move nothing in an atmosphere of mere natural sympathy and unbelief.

They all went to bed and I stayed, and that was surely a time as I knelt by that bed face to face with death and with the devil. But God can change the hardest situation and make you know that He is almighty.

Then the fight came. It seemed as though the heavens were brass. I prayed from 11:00 p.m. to 3:30 in the morning. I saw the glimmering light on the face of the sufferer and saw her pass away. The devil said, "Now you are done for. You have come from Bradford and the girl has died on your hands." I said, "It can't be. God did not send me here for nothing. This is a time to change strength." I remembered that passage which said, "Men ought always to pray and not to faint." Death had taken place but I knew that my God was all-powerful, and He that had split the Red Sea is just the same today. It was a time when I would not have "No," and God said "Yes." I looked at the window and at that moment the face of Jesus appeared. It seemed as though a million rays of light were coming from His face. As He looked at the one who had just passed away, the color came back to the face. She rolled over and fell asleep. Then I had a glorious time. In the morning she woke early, put on a dressing gown and walked to the piano. She started to play and to sing a wonderful song. The mother and the sister and the brother had all come down to listen. The Lord had undertaken. A miracle had been wrought.

The Lord is calling us along this way. I am thanking God for difficult cases. The Lord has called us into heart union with Himself; He wants His bride to have one heart and one Spirit with Him and to do what He Himself loved to do. That case had to be a miracle. The lungs were gone, they were just in shreds, but the Lord restored lungs that were perfectly sound.

The things which are impossible with men **are possible with God**. Lk. 18:27, KJV

RECOMMENDED READING

Visit http://www.smithwigglesworth.com/

By Smith Wigglesworth:

9

THE POWERFUL CHARACTER IN THE SUPERNATURAL DIMENSION

I

<u>Obedience to God in all circumstances</u>: this will make the power of God to do all, exceeding our expectancy and our knowledge. When Abraham obeyed to humiliate himself and his people, allowing another person to circumcise them, it made God to release to Abraham a special patriarchal anointing and he became the father

of nations and the covenant became sealed by his own blood and those of his people. Genesis 17

II

To rely on the power of God and expecting miracles: When Joshua was in the war against the enemy of God, he said something impossible to the understanding of men, to stop the Sun, in reality always the Sun is fixed, it doesn't move but by his determination of faith, the power was released to stop not the Sun but his influence to the earth to not turn around the Sun. It is unbelievable by that, the impossibility turns to possibility. The fight between David and Goliath was in the supernatural a war between the power of God and the satanic power. David by revelation knew it and he declared that I will defeat you by the name of God and it came to pass according his word. Here all the tools he could use would kill his enemy (1 Samuel 17: 42-52).

III

True love: The God we are serving is love and whatever we may do without the true love cannot be approved on the divine throne. Here we speak the language of forgiveness, the language of supporting each other, the language sharing the blessing and also to live in peace with others. God purpose is that his love be manifested amidst his people. Here we forget about race, color, nationality and all discriminations; we are one in the Lord, Jesus is our head, we are members of his body. When we fight among us we destroy his own body. Love is needed everywhere; I do not say that you will offer an occasion to expose yourself to your opponents. No, but when an occasion is offered to help them, do it with all your heart. Here, no insult, no gossip and no segregation. These characters will cause the power of God to move mightily in our lives and miracles shall rain amidst the people of God.

IV

Faith with Patience, Heart full of automatic worship, Positive prayers of authority

FAITH OF GOD WORKING IN US

The faith is not a matter of pretending, imitating or to impress others. It is a continuing connection with the Word of God; a) in thinking b) in speaking c) in behaving d) in inner attitudes e) in doing things

Nothing can be exempt from the control of God. He is in control and may change any difficult situation. He may create a good and better and best situation for those who grasp the truth of faith without complacency.

Therefore, I have to speak faith to eat, faith to exchange, faith to dwell in faith.

In Christ we are new creatures. Old things are passed away; behold, all things are become new (2Cor 5:17).

Many people are satisfied by the ordinary when God wants them to go beyond limitations. Satan fears your future more than your past but He tries to show you the failure of the past to keep you in bondage.

God told Moses to throw down his stick. After he said to him to take it again, it was not a stick but a serpent. It turns by miracle beyond his expectation. We also, as new creatures, had to throw out our philosophy, our empty tradition, our dead routine, our old way of dealing with things, and grasp the spiritual realm by faith.

The Word of God is your burning bush inside you and outside you.

Before you throw away your old fashioned attitudes, you cannot reach the transformation. God Himself transformed the staff to serpent and also the serpent to staff. Praise The Lord.

The connection you have to Jesus is worth more than your connections to humans; they are all sometimes unable to give a positive issue. They can kill you spiritually and physically because of their selfishness.

Only your faith will save your life long-term—relying on the word of God.

How many children of God are in several troubles because of relying on somebody?

Never rely totally on somebody else, including your traditional partner; sometimes trust can be displaced by untrust and all your life will be turned downward.

Faith is the hand that grasps the gift of God in Jesus and makes it our own.

To dwell in integrity in the Word of God will make us different.

This is the product of obeying the Word of God and not the emotion. Emotion is not the true reality; it is another way the devil utilizes to seduce the children of God so be aware of it and do not be led by emotions but by the Word of God.

Even if the emotion is so great, do not rush to act but rush to pray and go very deep in intercession. When you cannot stand, look for somebody who is strong in faith to agree with that person in the Word. Do this rather than turning to religion that will deceive you by improper compassion.

Psychology, philosophy, tradition, routine, never bring anointing or the presence of God at anytime.

The Word of God is one and unique for the transformation, miracle, healing, and for the anointing.

We have to close the door to these elements in our ministries and walk by faith and not by sight. We have to say faith, to dream faith, to eat faith, to digest faith and to manage everything by faith.

Today, many preachers are teaching psychology and their philosophy of thinking but that cannot replace the Word of God.

God is calling people to repent and to follow his instructions concerning dreams and destiny. If you do not have the dream of God in your life you will not reach the real destiny, that is, heaven. People like to be seduced by worldly words, by worldly philosophy, by worldly speeches. Paul said that his teaching and sermons were full of God's power. God is looking for the preachers who will tell this generation about His Son, about the repentance so He may heal the land.

Make Satan sad by telling everyone you meet what Jesus did for you and other adventures.

I decided not to watch on my television another actor if it is not Jesus. I do not have time to spend with foolish things that poison my intellect, my mind, and also my dream. What for? Even if many children of God like comedy, for me it is a waste of time.

The more I am connected to Jesus and to His Word, the more my faith flows and the more I am transformed by the holiness of God.

God is still in control, we have to accept the change by the transformation of our mind.

We must have faith to change our character, to heal our families and also our ministries.

There is no excuse for constant weakness; God gave us all that we need to perform what the situation requires.

If God didn't send Moses to Pharaoh, how could these Egyptians see the power of the God of Abraham?

If God didn't send Moses to the Red Sea, Israel would not have witnessed the greatness of God dividing water.

What can I say to the miracle of water, meat, manna, serpent, Jordan and the victories over Israel's enemies?

It is terrible if we wear ourselves to death fighting spiritual strongholds without God's power. "For though we walk in the flesh we do not war after the flesh: for the weapons of our warfare are not carnal, but mighty through God to the pulling down of strongholds: casting down imaginations, and every high thing that exalteth itself against the knowledge of God, and bringing into captivity every thought to the obedience of Christ;

II Cor. 10. 3-5

After Elijah predicted three years and six months of famine, he himself became affected by that situation. But God sent him to a location where his miracle provision would come through a raven that brought meat and bread every day till the brook dried up . . . (I Kings17:1-7).

We are not of them who draw back unto perdition; but of them that believe to the saving of the soul (Hebrews 10:38).

Your crisis is not for your destruction, it is for your elevation when you continue to wait joyfully for the Lord to move you up.

Don't go where others are going to look for security and care, using false and carnal strategies of Egypt. Your issue is in the hand of God. Your name is exalted in the high place even if nobody on this earth knows you.

Don't pretend to be what you aren't and want what you have not. Always submit to the Lord and resist the devil; he shall flee.

Faith chases away fear and doubt—it chases all that is against the will of God. It shakes the unseen into the realm of reality.

Faith is not an imitation but is an act, a step of obedience to the Word.

In time of trouble and insecurity please do not join with unbelief or join traditionally religious people. They may cause your spiritual death and even your physical death; find heroes of faith to be your associates and partners. Join me as I follow the Word of God.

Faith is different from religious dogma; it consists of taking the Lord at His word.

The true liberation is in your mouth, in your thoughts and strongly in your belief. As long you believe that the Lord Jesus set you free, you don't have to doubt your freedom.

That freedom cost Him His life, His freedom, and His blood.

He was a prisoner that we may not be under any kind of slavery.

When the Son of God makes you free you are free indeed.

John 8:36

So do not sell your freedom, your dignity, your personality though you pass through fire. Have faith in God and do not authorize anybody to use you for material gain. If you do, you will be a slave of this one and you may become a slave to his vision. Why allow anybody else to decide on your destiny? Who is he? If it means to starve, better to do it than to be a slave of somebody. God already delivered us. Why sacrifice your soul for a loaf of bread? It may cause you to lose your destiny.

Your words can heal you or kill you, so you can become the worst enemy of your own destiny.

Even when you encounter a very overwhelming situation, don't try to be whatever your body tends to dictate. Be what the Word of God says: say it, believe it, and proclaim it.

Do not be surprised when some so-called ministers may tell you the opposite of your faith.

Faith is a process, and action is an achiever. Know that it is personal and not from outside. It is inside you, so nobody can believe in your place. You have to persist till you reach your destination.

Even when things are delayed, it does not necessarily mean no. Wait by faith till you touch the point where God wants you.

The Lord Jesus told his disciples to go off by themselves while he went to pray on the mountain.

He knew that they would arrive at the destination, but in the middle of their journey, wind and storms disturbed their security and their trip. Jesus was praying. As the night continued and the danger escalated, the disciples reached a catastrophic moment.

At that very moment, the Lord came walking on the water; the disciples thought that it was their end, meeting a ghost.

It was not—instead it was the time of solution.

We will not discuss at the moment Peter's walk on the water at the order of Jesus. We do read that the Lord spoke with the wind, knowing that the cause of the storm was the wind. Immediately, the storm ceased and security was re-established.

The Lord Jesus is our security whatever dark valley we cross.

Without the situation I face today, I will not be what God wants me to be tomorrow. Praise God all the time. He knows the very next step and He has a good plan for you. A plan of hope, of joy, of dignity, of elevation, of reparation, of glory, of healing and salvation.

By faith your miracle is being released and it will knock on your door by faith. Faith is all we need in such times.

Let doubts and unbelief go far from you; you don't need them. You need a true deliverance by the Word not by your roller coaster emotions.

Believe and go free in the name of Jesus.

There is no true deliverance if it does not come from the incorruptible Word of God.

When Lazarus did four days in the tomb, Jesus came; He spoke to death to release him and it came to pass. All things are possible for those who believe. If you do not believe, you cannot see the glory of God.

To believe is the decision of the now and to refuse belongs to you.

We have to grasp faith to cast down our pride, our knowledge, our philosophy and old thoughts. We must become humble before the Lord so He can bring a restoration of what we have in a new dimension.

This step will cause miracles to hit our ministries, the transformation of our families and situations.

God told Moses to throw down his shepherd staff that was his instrument of work. When he did, it was transformed and he feared to take it again because it became a snake. But by the order of God he took it again and it returned to its original form. Praise The Lord.

Why destroy your destiny by holding to vain fashions and traditions.

Selfishness, self esteem, pretence, trying to make impressions and all sorts of alienations such as these do not come from God.

This is vanity and makes somebody a charlatan.

Be strong in faith and be true and honest in your walk with God.

Sometimes your faith may cause you to pass through the fire but this fire will never consume you (**Isaiah 43:2).**

Peter sat in jail, awaiting the sentence of death. Instead, he saw an angel who was ordered by the counsel from above to deliver Him.

The counsel from above is in our favor and not against us, so rejoice because of this right and declaration.

Paul and Silas in jail saw the glory of God, and the counsel on high made an order to deliver them: An angel came to untie them and to open the door of the jail. Glory to God.

I am so excited and I bless the Lord who made me an heir of the treasures of heaven.

The situation you face today is not for long term; it is for a short time.

Loose your faith to go out and face that situation, you have the favor of the high court. You are not guilty. You are free, go in peace in Jesus' name.

You are healed in Jesus' name.

You are saved by believing in Jesus Christ.

As long you will work by the principles of God, your economy shall dwell strong and unshakable by the enemy.

Pay your tithe constantly, give your offerings and alms, and worship the Lord. Read the word of God. Walk in faith, talk faith, plant your seeds in all the situations that God has authorized.

Keep your mouth clear of junk words, your eyes from junky pictures, your ears from vanity, and you shall live here strong and you surely have the promise to reach the new heaven and the New Jerusalem.

That is a good end. Holiness is the nature of God, so grasp it for long term and not only in the church. It is your guarantee to enter into heaven. Your brief moment of personal glory may cause your eternal shame. Take care and do not play or joke with God. He is not the joker but a fulfiller of his promises.

If some leaders who didn't deal with Jesus could stand by their position and finally reach their destiny, how much more shall you and I? Those without Jesus are struggling only with world causes, but the children of God have the promise both here and in heaven.

Some political leaders stood on what they believed till they received the earthly desire of their heart. The children of God have strong reasons to move on and do far better than these.

Now faith is the substance of things hoped for, the evidence of things not yet seen.

But without faith it is impossible to please God: for he that comes to God must believe that He is . . . (**Hebrew.11: 1&6**).

When you open your mouth please say what you believe and it will come to pass by the power of God.

Instead of speaking non-stop words of unbelief, better to be quiet and to meditate upon the power of God. If you do not open your mouth, nobody else will force you. Why curse and condemn yourself by your own words?

"Then you are trapped by your own words, and you are now in the power of someone else . . ." (**Prov.6:2**).

For your advantage, declare faith, dream faith, and show faith, though you do not feel, see, or touch the reality yet. Don't worry, it will come to pass. The longer you believe, the easier it will become to transform the unseen to the seen. Trust God with all your heart; Jesus is the healer. There is abundant healing in faith through Jesus. You can project it into all situations. Jesus is the doer of miracles; believe it and live.

Don't fall victim to the unbelief of certain religious people who deny the power of the gospel. When we quote God, power is behind him at all times. Don't be deceived.

Be always edified by the Word of God and not the words of people.

Words of people may be good but not true; that is the difference.

The Word of God may seem difficult but it has life inside it.

Do not authorize your past to steal your blessings.

We both passed by many mess ups, but now we have a clear vision.

The past is past; let's continue with a real experience by faith.

Apostle Paul said that "I have not yet reached my goal, and I am not perfect. But Christ has taken a hold of me. So, I keep on running and struggling to take hold of the prize . . . I don't feel that I have already arrived. But I forget what is behind, and I struggle for what is ahead. I run toward the goal, so that I can win the prize of being called to heaven" (**Phil.3:12-14**).

Brethren, we cannot walk by feelings and experience the miracles of God, neither can we know the power of the resurrection.

It is true that we are new creatures; this cannot be understood by our intellect but by the spirit in faith.

For though we walk in the flesh, we do not war after the flesh: for the weapons of our warfare are not carnal, but mighty through God . . .

(2 Cor.10:2-3).

It is nonsense to join people who cannot help you, but the word of faith in the time of trouble is enough to lift you up.

The leader who doesn't obey the "thus saith the Lord" always leads people into self-destruction.

Moses did follow all the instructions of God without complacency, thus bringing Israel from Egypt to the desert.

Joshua did follow the steps of Moses and success followed him.

We do not need the strange fire; those we have in God's storage is strong enough for anybody and everybody.

Pharaoh heard the Word of God but despised it and the result was the destruction of himself and his people.

God never told Pharaoh to enter the Red Sea. That was for Moses and Israel.

My miracle is mine; if you try to steal it, you will destroy your destiny.

All the times you provoke me, you are provoking the anger of God toward you. I will not take revenge but He will, and He cannot forget.

I know to whom I will talk no matter what bad things you say to or about me. No matter what treatment you do to me, my defender lives.

The body of Christ has a great need to change, to be transformed so we can grasp the spiritual realities.

We need the change of the paradigm of life to a paradigm of faith that simply takes God at his Word.

Change of mentality (to move out of carnal routine)

Change of priorities.

Change of system focusing on heaven's benefits.

Change of conception—ability to see as giants.

I don't care how you preach, how many people you have, or your gift. Your talent can bring you to a place where your character cannot keep you right. Unless you present your body as a pleasing sacrifice to God, a problem will dwell in your life. Let your body glorify the Lord. The daily fight you have is against the lust of the flesh and the lust of eyes. Our total victory depends on how we surrender our life to satisfy the will of God and not of the flesh.

Adultery and immorality will never be supported by God.

Men and women of God have the faith to build a palace and buy anything they conceive. That may be good, but it is not enough; they must have faith to keep themselves pure and clean before the Lord.

How can you neglect your relationship with God and pretend to be a winner? How can you neglect your relations with your family and claim to be right? How can you neglect the care of the ministry and claim to be the disciple of Jesus?

In the name of the Lord, let me tell you today that your faith did not tell you to wear sexy clothes. That is a lie of the devil. He is in the business of manufacturing a vast array of seductions. They stand as a snare, causing us to sin in the spirit. Be a Christian inside and outside and be not subject to give sin an occasion to crush you.

What we see today is subject to change so it is strongly recommended that we invest in the kingdom of God.

So much is on our minds: Faith, times, money, vision and plans.

Do not invest your heart in corruptible things but incorruptible.

Shake the unshakable by the power of the Holy Spirit.

Every child of God has inside him the power to transform his environment.

The strategy is not to try to change people but to be changed first.

Change is a process; it is not a magical tactic. It is done by faith and by your decision.

Let's walk according to the new creation.

Don't be comfortable with old things.

The time we spent in turning around the mountain is enough.

We have to press by faith to our destiny.

If you know where you are going, be sure that by perseverance you will reach your destination.

Privation and Sacrifice, To always remain in the presence of God, you must hate to violate the will of God

This testimony is strong enough to convince all children of God to avoid violating the will of God and to keep on believing his elevation.

***JUST LIKE A PRAYER . . . Kaka looks to the heavens after winning
the Champions League with Milan***

*KAKA may be the man to fire Manchester City to glory but that would be
nothing compared to the impact he has already has had on millions of people*

*The AC Milan star has given the green light to a staggering £243million
switch to Eastlands. But the Brazilian says football plays second fiddle in a
life which has been devoted to Christianity.*

*Just weeks ago he became involved with the Billy Graham organization in
a TV campaign which had an astonishing effect in his homeland. It was
nationally reported that:*

Hundreds of people were freed from demonic possession.

*Hardened criminals turned to Christianity by the thousands. Many more
were cured of booze and drug addictions. A former voodoo princess turned
to Christ.*

*As the campaign launched, Kaka told millions: "I truly cannot imagine my
life without Christ.*

"Everything I have accomplished, everything I have done in my life was because God has a plan and purpose for my life.

"The Bible says He will do more than we ever thought or imagined, and this is truly how it has been. If God wasn't in my life, then my life certainly would not be like this."

The Brazilian's faith in God has been broadcast throughout the world via an iconic picture of him on his knees celebrating a goal and showing a T-shirt which proclaims, 'I belong to Jesus.'

Kaka, age 26, has won a World Cup in the Champions League as well as being named FIFA World Player of the Year.

But he told 10 million fellow Brazilians that nothing compared with the peace of knowing and serving Christ.

He said: "I have been named best soccer player in the world. This for me was a great honour. But the greatest honour is serving Jesus Christ, because he gives me hope."

Such is the depth of the star's faith he refused to have sex before his marriage to Caroline.

He said: "I am a great example. The majority of people say that after marriage, they don't like jumping into bed with their partner because there is no desire. However, this is not true, my wife is the person I love and it was worth waiting. A lot of people were surprised and shocked with me but I think it's the best decision. I am an evangelist and I believe in those values.

"I think people need to prevent themselves from making love before marriage. Everyone has their opinion but I think it was worth the wait."

The Brazilian's faith in the Almighty was strengthened immensely in the year 2000 when he fractured his neck after cracking his head on the bottom of a swimming pool. Kaka said: "That helped shape me, principally as a person, but as a player too.

"It was a time in which I learned you have to give your best every single day because the next day you might not be able.

"The doctors said I was very lucky, that I could have been paralyzed. But I think it was God—He saved me from something worse.

"I had gone to visit my grandparents in Caldas Novas in Brazil and I slipped on a swimming pool slide.

"When I fell into the water I hit my head on the bottom of the pool and twisted my neck, which caused a fracture of a vertebra.

"All I knew was that anyone with a broken neck would be disabled for life. The doctor told me I would not be able to play for at least three months; then they would be able to tell if I was going to fully recover.

"But after two months the injury had healed and I was able to resume my football career. That was when I knew God was looking after me and that He was on my side."

Kaka says one of the chief influences on his footballing life has been Chelsea boss, Phil Scolari.

He said: "When I was just 20 he took me to the World Cup in 2002 and gave me the opportunity to be a champion, which was very important."

And Kaka believes if he is to move to City, it will be thanks to a higher power.

He said: "If things happen it's because God has prepared me. God has great things for us. If it's God's will that I be there, there I will be."

V

CONFESSION AND DECLARATION OF VICTORY BASED ON THE WORDS OF GOD.

Confessing, Meditating, and bearing the promises of God will put you in a secure place and it is very helpful to validate your potentiality.

There is enough potential of power in each human being regardless of his origin.

No matter your color or your nationality and race, together we have enough potential to achieve and to grow spiritually in an excellent environment.

Some people have a house as the main goal in their minds. If they concentrate all their power on eventually purchasing a house, there's a good chance they will get it one day.

The ambition you have in your vision can enable you to release enough power or energy to become the kind of man or woman you see in your dream.

No matter what people think about you, you are responsible for your vision.

If for some reason you are surrounded by people who are there to discourage you, leave them and go your way alone. These people should be considered as a poison to deviate you and to block your power to react.

Because of this power you will be able to make a plan and organize yourself to be what you saw in your dream. God does not create a useless human. He never did a useless activity.

You cannot be a hero if you do not know how to defend what you are doing, your dream and your total life purpose.

No need for people to accept totally your vision, they cannot, but you yourself have to accept it 100%. You have a design and a picture inside you others do not have.

Most of the time, incapable people think that everybody is like them. Be yourself and do not be intimidated by the crowd.

There are a multitude of people who want to hear you and your inspiration. Be busy with them. Invest your talents in them. It is your experimental field to you and your crown.

Do not focus your attention to someone who despises you, even if it is your father, your mother, your son and anyone else. Love them, help them if they are in need, but do not authorize them to destroy your destiny. The friend of your vision is your true brother.

Jesus said that his mother and his brothers are those who do the will of His Father. This means those who support and follow his vision and purpose for why He came.

It is useless to waste your time with people who reject your destiny.

If somebody cannot encourage your vision or assist you, he is useless to you at this time, better to say goodbye, and continue on your way.

Success will bring them all, perhaps with tears and an apology.

There is power in you that some people cannot see properly. They think you are pretending, that's ok. They do not know you really. God knows you and He believes in what you are doing to subdue the earth. The disciples of Jesus, who before were cowards, arrived at a specific moment in which they released the power inside them and the gospel of Jesus reached the four corners of the earth. These disciples such as Peter, John and Andrew, etc . . . were fishermen without the ambition to be celebrities, but when they released the power inside them for what they believed, a big transformation came. They had a name because of the releasing of the power inside them.

You do not have to force people to believe in you, but your perseverance and your faith will cause them to accept and to join your vision.

The mocker of yesterday will be the disciple of tomorrow.

Be courageous and sincere, your ticket for success is already printed.

Everybody has to activate the power inside them by faith. This means that two basic elements must be activated to succeed. The first one is faith and the second is the power.

These are the chief principles of winners.

VI

The Joy and Assurance of Heaven

HEAVEN IS NOT FOR LEASE

HEAVEN IS NOT FOR RENT

HEAVEN IS NOT FOR LOAN

HEAVEN IS FOR WINNERS

PEOPLE WASHED BY THE BLOOD OF JESUS

PEOPLE WHO FIGHT WITH GOD'S WEAPONS

HEAVEN IS NOT A STORY; IT IS A REALITY

IT IS A CHOICE TO WANT IT AND A CHOICE TO BE SANCTIFIED AND PURIFIED BY THE BLOOD OF THE LAMB.

PREACHERS, PLEASE DO NOT DRAW PEOPLE TO LOVE THE WORLD AND ALL THAT IT CONTAINS. ALL IN IT IS TEMPORARY AND FAKE. THE PERMANENT JOY AND TRUE HAPPINESS DWELL IN HEAVEN.

DEAR BROTHER, FIGHT THE GOOD FIGHT; GOD KNOWS THAT YOU WERE A LIAR BUT YOU ARE NOT STILL THERE.

GOD KNOWS THAT YOU WERE AN ADULTERER BUT YOU ARE NOT STILL THERE. GOD KNOWS THAT YOU WERE A TROUBLE MAKER BUT YOU ARE NOT STILL THERE. YOU REPENTED OF ALL THE WORST SORT OF BEHAVIOUR AND YOU ARE CALLED A VIRGIN BY GOD'S JUSTICE. REJOICE BECAUSE YOU ARE KNOWN IN HEAVEN, THOUGH YOUR NAME IS UNKNOWN IN YOUR ENVIRONMENT. THAT IS NOTHING; YOU ARE THE PROPERTY OF CHRIST AND A PRIEST UNTO GOD.

> [15]Love not the world, neither the things that are in the world. If any man love the world, the love of the Father is not in him.
>
> [16]For all that is in the world, the lust of the flesh, and the lust of the eyes, and the pride of life, is not of the Father, but is of the world.

[17]And the world passeth away, and the lust thereof: but he that doeth the will of God abideth for ever.

[18]Little children, it is the last time: and as ye have heard that antichrist shall come, even now are there many antichrists; whereby we know that it is the last time.

[19]They went out from us, but they were not of us; for if they had been of us, they would no doubt have continued with us: but they went out, that they might be made manifest that they were not all of us.

[20]But ye have an unction from the Holy One, and ye know all things.

"Blessed are they that are called unto the marriage supper of the Lamb." And he said unto me, "These are the true sayings of God."

VII

Wisdom to plant the seed of faith

[19]Lay not up for yourselves treasures upon earth, where moth and rust doth corrupt, and where thieves break through and steal:

[20]But lay up for yourselves treasures in heaven, where neither moth nor rust doth corrupt, and where thieves do not break through nor steal:

[21]For where your treasure is, there will your heart be also.

Ecclesiastes 11

[4]He that observeth the wind shall not sow; and he that regardeth the clouds shall not reap.

⁵As thou knowest not what is the way of the spirit, nor how the bones do grow in the womb of her that is with child: even so thou knowest not the works of God who maketh all.

⁶In the morning sow thy seed, and in the evening withhold not thine hand: for thou knowest not whether it shall prosper, either this or that, or whether they both shall be alike good.

PSALMS, 126

⁵They that sow in tears shall reap in joy.

⁶He that goeth forth and weepeth, bearing precious seed, shall doubtless come again with rejoicing, bringing his sheaves with him.

VIII

Be original and not a copy

"Why do we have such conflicts in the world today? It is because the world is filled with people infected by an irresponsible spirit: sin. The world's irresponsibility carries with it a sense of lacking conscience or being unable or unwilling to respond to conscience. It is the conscience that allows us to distinguish between right and wrong."—MYLES MUNROE

The time for playing religious is over. The days are short. For the first time in our generation, religious wars are taking center stage. Increasingly religion will be seen as one of the problems in our world. What can we do when both religion and government are powerless to solve our problems? We must put our trust in something that no man can penetrate. What we need is an alternative kingdom, a government that only Jesus can bring.

Isaiah; 9: 6-7 For to us a child is born, to us a son is given, and the government will be upon his shoulders. And He will be called Wonderful, Counselor, Mighty God, Everlasting Father, and Prince of peace.

The world needs peace. It needs hope and security. And these can be found only in the kingdom of God. We have assurance of God's provision, but we are to seek first His Kingdom and His righteousness and all these things will be given to us (Matt 6: 33).

God is calling the Church together in unity. Believers in home cell groups, communities and churches must continue in prayer and oneness.

We cannot change the past but we can determine the quality of our future. When we choose to obey the ways of The Lord, He will back us up. It is time to pray.

God didn't ordain governments to be the salt of the earth. He ordained you and me to be the preservative influence on the earth.

Criticism doesn't change anything. Prayer does.

Times of crisis and tragedy are not the time to fix the blame on anyone.

What really makes life worth living is not what we have; it is the love we share with people.

Every road may look good, but only one will be right.

God is still on the throne. He has not moved an inch. He is not on vacation and He has not left town. He is not traumatized by events on earth. He is not in therapy, and He has not retired. He is fit and well, and He reigns as the supreme, indisputable King of the universe. God is not subnormal and He is not abnormal. He is not old normal or new normal. He is super normal. So what are doing looking anywhere else?

Many talk of Him loudly as if He is present, but secretly they think of Him as being absent.

If you are walking with God, it doesn't matter who comes against you or who you go against; you will always win. But if you are not walking with HIM, it doesn't matter how small the enemy is; you will always be defeated (Deuteronomy 28).

I think that in this generation we have lost a fear of God. We have made a god in our own image

For I KNOW that my redeemer lives, and that he shall stand at the latter day upon the earth (JOB 19: 25).

Behold, I will send you corn, and wine, and oil, and ye shall be satisfied therewith . . . And ye shall eat in plenty, and be satisfied, and praise the name of The Lord your God, that hath dealt wondrously with you; AND MY PEOPLE SHALL NOT BE ASHAMED (Joel 2; 19, 26).

They that know thy name will put their trust in thee: for thou, Lord, has not (never) forsaken them that seek thee (Psalm 9.9-10).

Surely He shall DELIVER ME from the snare of the fowler, and from the noisome pestilence. He shall cover thee with his feathers, and under his wings shall thou trust; his truth shall be thy shield and buckled (Psalm 91: 3-4)

Yea, though I walk through the valley of the shadow of death, I will fear no evil: for thou art with me; thy rod and thy staff they comfort me (Psalm 23: 4).

My flesh and my heart faileth: but God is the strength of my heart, and my portion forever (Psalm 73: 26).

When a man's ways please yhe Lord, he makes even his enemies to be at peace with him (Pr 16: 7).

The Lord knoweth how to deliver the godly out of the temptation. (2peter2:9).

They that wait upon the Lord shall renew their strength; they shall mount up with wings as eagles; they shall run, and not be weary; and they shall walk, and not faint (Isaiah 40:31).

The Lord is my rock, and my fortress, and my deliverer; my God, my strength, in Whom I will trust; my buckler, and the horn of my salvation, and my tower (Psalm 18:2).

1John 2.15-18 Love not the world, neither the things that are in the world. If any man love the world, the love of the father is not in him. For all that is in the world, the lust of the flesh, and the lust of the eyes, and the pride of life, is not of the Father, but is of the world. And the world passeth away, and the lust thereof: but he that doeth the will of God abides forever. Little children, it is the last time: and as ye have heard that anti-christ shall come, even now are there many antichrists: whereby we know that it is the last time.

BE BUSY WITH YOUR INSIDE AND GOD WILL BE BUSY ON THE OUTSIDE

Nobody could understand what he saw, what he heard, what he constantly stated. It was a shaking of the world, dead were raised up, trees were dried up by His word, winds stopped blowing, he caused the blind to see, demons left people, bread and fishes were mysteriously multiplied. It was a brand new thing, a different thing when the Lord Jesus came to earth.

God visited the earth but the people who were supposed to work for Him refused Him. That's because their hearts were foolish by nature and they were filled with the empty desires of the world; they were friends of the world. They could not discern the will of God and His power.

Jesus is still alive, ready to revive us in holiness and power, in healing and in restoring all that Satan took from us.

Let people who laugh at you continue to laugh. But the visitation of God will close their mouths as it describes in Mark 5:40-43. Be prepared for the elevation of God and do not put your trust in anybody. Things can change anytime. Be wise and do not be deceived; Jesus is all that we need, worth more than all the names you may think worthy. Thank you, Jesus.

For I know the thoughts that I think toward you, saith the Lord, thoughts of peace and not of evil, to give you an expected end Then shall ye call upon me and you shall go and pray unto me, and I will hearken unto you. And you shall seek me, and find me, when you shall search for me with all your heart. And I will be found of you, saith the Lord; and I will turn away your captivity, and I will gather you from all the nations, and from all the places whither I have driven you, saith the Lord.

(Jeremiah 29 11-14)

The good news is that God does not abandon us in our time of need. "As sure as God puts His CHILDREN in the furnace of affliction," said Charles Spurgeon, "He will be with them in it."

Nobody can help me to activate my faith if I don't want it. Nobody can help me to speak, to praise the Lord, to read my Bible, to plant the seed of faith, nobody can believe in my place.

I shall do my part and God will do His part. I don't know how to produce miracles but I know how to keep my faith which will cause God to be pleased and do the miraculous. Sure I know what it means. Jeremiah 29: 11 states that He has plans of peace and He promises me hope and a future. I refuse to accept the opposite of that statement because God is not a man that He should lie. That is my address, and it works. What I need is faith in God, believing His Word, and I declare today that my destiny is accomplished by faith. What is your dream within your heart? If you do not have one, then just follow mine and respect my plan and vision till you receive blessings from it. You need more than what you have, trust God and forget all defeat in your life. Arise, your faith has healed you. Neither distance nor time can block God from giving you the best. Keep on believing God. Tradition and routine are killing us. Arise, Jesus is alive. We need fresh bread for today; we need the revelation and discernment. Don't force people to understand you, your persistence in faith will convince them in time and will prove your value to those outside. Remain inside till God occupies the outside. Distraction brings deception and uncontrolled deceptions drive one to confusion and multiple distractions, so flee any sort of distraction, lust, philosophy, criticism, all works of flesh cannot free you and you can never be the friend of God and the world. Jesus died that the blessing of Ibrahim be unto me, my family, and my business. All battles are not mine but God's, who in the new covenant will curse those who curse me and bless those who bless me. I am not a failure even if I don't see my destiny today.

I see my victory by faith, my future elevation and all my expectations.

Praise the name of Jesus. The peace that God gives is in the family, in the work, in the ministry, in the spirit and in difficult things. Even if my situation gets worse, I have to believe in that peace and resist Satan in all areas of my life so I can call on the Lord with a pure heart and I will look for his face and find Him.

Nothing will stop me from believing in an expected future and from keeping hold of that glorious hope. All that Satan is showing you is deception, discouragement and despair. Don't trust the devil; trust God with all your heart. All chosen servants of God passed through the fire but God never forsook them and they all arrived at the destination in spite of the trials. God is using your actual circumstances to prove to you His power. I don't need the miracle of yesterday; I want what is now. The way may have many difficulties and obstacles, but the end of it will make you forget all the worries. Know that we have a country to conquer, Canaan, and souls to bring into the kingdom of God.

IX

Holiness and Fear of the Lord

<u>1 Peter 1:</u> [15]But as he which hath called you is holy, so be ye holy in all manner of conversation;

[16]Because it is written, Be ye holy; for I am holy.

The Fear of The Lord

Genesis 15.1
Ex 1.21 25.17
Numbers 14.9
Deuteronomy 1.22

Joshua 8.1 4.14
Luke 2.10 12.5
Deuteronomy 10.12-13
Isaiah 8.13
The fear of circumstances will enslave me but the fear of the Lord is the
    beginning of wisdom
        Jeremiah 27; 5 Proverbs 29:25p
If the foundation is destroyed what can the righteous do? (Prov. 11:3)
Weeping may endure for a night but joy comes in the morning
    (Psalm 33:5b).

Many times God allows His chosen people to pass through an undesirable situation in order to manifest His power. Joseph and Mary wished to deliver Jesus in a good hotel but God prepared a broken down shack for that.

Angels and Wise men and shepherds came to worship Jesus at the same place. The star of glory was fixed at that place. Angels came down and danced at that place. Heaven came down. Even Joseph and Mary didn't realize that fact.

Abraham went to Egypt. Isaac did too. Joseph went to Egypt. Moses, too, stood before a Pharaoh and a prince became a shepherd. Accept the place where God put you; it is for a season. Everything shall pass and there will come a day for your elevation. Humble yourself before God. He will elevate you for the coming day.

God decided the death of His own Son to result in our salvation. Satan rejoiced to have Him in his dominion, but He went down to conquer and was raised up a great conqueror. Death and Hades had a short moment of feast because the light appeared where darkness had taken dominion. He took the key from Satan and delivered captives. Praise The Lord.

They had stripped him naked and beaten Him like a murderer, but it only lasted for a few hours. Someday every tongue shall confess Jesus is Lord and every knee shall bow of things on high, things on earth, and things under the earth shall bow before Him. Who you are and where you are and what you are do not give you a guarantee, but your identity in Christ is your success and your guarantee. Change occurs at times while we're still in the battle. Even when we were sometimes stuck we were still in the kingdom. Even when we do not have well known names here in the world our names are known in heaven and written in the book of life. And one day we shall become as purified gold. God is God before His manifestation of deliverance. To have a faulty knowledge of God will give power to Satan to confuse you. God is God and He remains good, the forgiver, powerful, omnipresent, omniscient, omnipotent Father of the fatherless, defender of widows, my rock, my fortress, my buckler, my redeemer, my father, my reason to live, my daily food, my secret weapon, my subject of joy, my personal friend, my great I am, my everything. Moses, the chosen servant of God, enjoyed forty years in the kingdom palace as a prince. Because of the purpose of God, He became a lowly shepherd for forty years. Not for one month, not one year but . . . . after he did forty years alone in the wilderness he was troubled by his proper people.

When churches are filled with people nursing spiritual pride, the blessings of community are overshadowed by ugly competition. They become places where we compete with one another, trying to impress others with our spiritual maturity. Confession is difficult in this context because to confess is to shatter our fantasized persona of perfection. But we must not resist genuine confession

Confession involves sacrificing our good image for the sake of truth or a relationship with another. Because confession has a cost, we often resist it (Psalm 55.17-20).

To be the victim in a Situation

Anybody can be victim in a critical situation, whether he or she is faithful or not. But that situation is temporary; God Himself will take care of it if you focus your eyes on him. Many misunderstandings occur when people are in a critical situation. God remains God and He shall deliver His people in good time: Joseph, Moses, Elijah, Samuel, Raha (2Peter 2.9). Weeping may remain for a night, but rejoicing comes the morning (Psalm 30:5).

If the foundations be destroyed what can the righteous do? (Psalm 11: 3)

Don't accuse God for your lack of knowledge. He is faithful; He is not a liar. What He said He will do, He shall. My sins, my transgressions put me in conflict against God, I have to repent and not repeat. When I gossiped, when I cheated, when I failed to tithe, when I lied, when I feared to confess the name of Jesus, He was watching me. Joseph said to Potiphar's wife, "I cannot offend God and your husband." When we walk with God it is sure that He shall manifest His power to deliver, to heal, to promote, to secure, to give an expected end. The desire of your heart, God wants to give it to you (Romans 3:4).

Many among us are prisoners of their past, prisoners of the words of people. Be free by the Word of God, accept the mercy God offered you through Jesus. Move on and forget the mistakes of your past. Whoever the Son makes free is free indeed. The past has passed, the future is for your restoration. Today is an opportunity for making the decision to accept God's voice or people's voices. A majority cannot replace the style or the Word of God.

We are not among those who perish even when we seem to be in a critical situation. Weeping may endure the night but joy comes in the morning. Even if God promised blessings to Abraham he didn't enjoy the trials that accompanied them. He faced many difficult situations but he never quit. The same was true for Moses, Joshua, Samuel, David, Joseph, Peter, and all the disciples of Jesus, even Mary (Heb.10:37).

We will enjoy many things about the life in Jesus but also we must be prepared to suffer for Him. Sometimes we pray and we feel that God is not listening to us but He never minimizes nor forgets the prayer of His just. We are not the quitters; we are those who saved their souls by faith in the Christ (Hebrews 10:38). It is impossible to please God without faith and nothing can be done without prayers, true love, true sacrifices and giving.

10

DO NOT SUPERNATURALIZE YOUR FAMILY RESPONSIBILITIES

Although you are used powerfully in the ministry or any outside matters, do not neglect to perform your marital responsibilities. Do you think that you shall kiss your husband or your wife in heaven? Do you think you will have the good times with your loved one in heaven? In heaven there is no man and woman—no marriage as such. God gives us to enjoy our honeymoon here on earth; in heaven it is another world. Do your best to be a true blessing and a real soul mate to your partner. Nobody else can give that joy to each other; all must be done in the marriage. It is God's command to give up your body to your partner and put away the idea of abusing each other in the area of intimacy.

Many powerful men and women forget to ask for the wisdom of God to deal with their loved ones. We have to know that our partners in our families have the right to see us, to communicate and to share love. If you forget to kiss your loved one, who else will do it for you? You may be much occupied on the outside till you forget the first seed you have to take care of. Your wife needs you, your husband needs you and your children need you. Do not imagine that to spend time with your loved one will withdraw your anointing; this is a big mistake and the reason for many divorces in the camp of the priesthood.

A servant of God has to reserve a time to teach his only family and to correct his children in the will of God. Isaac, the son of Abraham our father of faith, had a good time touching his wife, Rebekah, and reciprocally. They did not hide their love till the King of Egypt reached out his hands to Rebekah.

Genesis 26

[8]And it came to pass, when he had been there a long time, that Abimelech king of the Philistines looked out at a window, and saw, and, behold, Isaac was sporting with Rebekah his wife.

[9]And Abimelech called Isaac, and said, Behold, of a surety she is thy wife; and how saidst thou, She is my sister? And Isaac said unto him, Because I said, Lest I die for her.

[10]And Abimelech said, What is this thou hast done unto us? One of the people might lightly have lien with thy wife, and thou shouldest have brought guiltiness upon us.

[11]And Abimelech charged all his people, saying, 'He that toucheth this man or his wife shall surely be put to death.'

[12]Then Isaac sowed in that land, and received in the same year an hundredfold: and the LORD blessed him.

LOVE IS LIFE AND NOT A STRANGE STORY

Love is not in words but in actions
Love is who you are deep inside
Love is not only what you think but what you do
Love is not a dream; it is the reality
Love is not a mystery but visible actions and reactions
Love must be shared and is not selfish
Love looks at the benefit for another human being
Love brings joy amidst sorrows
Love is needed everywhere
Love is the solution forever
Love is a living light in the heart, the spirit and the soul
Love is incomparable, and you need it now
Love is a remedy without medicine
Love is not only the desire of the flesh
Love is the heart speaking sincerity
Love is not lust but a precious gift
Love doesn't carry death but produces life
Love is the fundamental answer of inner need
Love fills the cup of satisfaction
Love is the container of good surprises
Love doesn't look for the mistake but for reparation
Love never counts the number of mess ups
Love is new everyday and it forgets the past
Love brings hope even in the desert
Love itself is life and hope
Love always gives another opportunity
Faith can never replace love
Hope can never replace love
Corruption can never replace love
God is love
I LOVE YOU

Dr. RAHA MUGISHO

2009/02/24 11:59

106

People have to stop with cold "religious" prayer and worship and enter deeply in spiritual adoration, banishing all vain words which reflect a lack of faith, knowing that without faith it is impossible to please God. Your holiness is hidden in your faith because in the true faith abide holiness and God's love; without faith there is no true holiness. If you are not receiving answers to prayer something must be wrong in the matter of faith. That is the reason the Word of God says, 'without faith it is impossible to please God.'

Your possession, your title and your position must kneel before God, not only your spirit. The way you think is what you are. Put the Word of God first; the promises of God are yours. Confess the Word in all circumstances and you will not be ashamed if you truly believe.

God didn't send anybody to destroy the sinners or the backsliders but to bring them to the light, using His love and compassion. We are not traveling with the names of backsliders but the name of Jesus. If I want to deal with such things, the Bible tells me to meet the person and talk with him, to show him the truth and pray for him and not to reject or to curse him. That is the mistake that many religious men do and it destroys not the devil, but the work of God.

Mark 9: 23 IF YOU CAN ALL THINGS IS POSSIBLE . . .